School Libraries and Student Learning

School Libraries and Student Learning

A Guide for School Leaders

Rebecca J. Morris

Harvard Education Press
Cambridge, Massachusetts

Library of Congress Control Number 2015937063

Paperback ISBN 978-1-61250-836-8
Library Edition ISBN 978-1-61250-837-5

Published by Harvard Education Press,
an imprint of the Harvard Education Publishing Group

Harvard Education Press
8 Story Street
Cambridge, MA 02138

Cover Design: Wilcox Design
Cover Photo: © Hero Images Inc./Corbis
The typefaces used in this book are Adobe Garamond Pro and ITC Legacy Sans.

CONTENTS

1 School Libraries for Today's Learners 1

2 Makerspaces and Learning Commons 31
Supporting Student-Centered Learning

3 Reading Across the Curriculum 57
Fostering Literacy and Transliteracy Skills

4 Inquiry and Critical Thinking 83
Transforming the Culture of Learning

5 Assessment for Learning 103
Partnering with Teachers and Students

6 Responding to Diverse Needs 125
Authentic Engagement with Families and Communities

7 Practical Matters 147
Schedules, Technology, Evaluation, and More

8 Excellence for Libraries, Excellence for Schools 171
School Libraries and Student Learning

Appendix: School Library Checklist 185

Notes 191

Acknowledgments 203

About the Author 205

Index 207

For my parents, John and Annette—

You are models of love and giving.

For my brother, Jim—

You teach me to be strong in so many ways.

For Brian—You are my heart.

CHAPTER 1

School Libraries for Today's Learners

DO WE STILL NEED a school library? Are school libraries keeping up with changes in education? Is a school library worth the space and funding? The answer to all of these questions is an emphatic *yes*! We need school libraries because they can help schools achieve important priorities.

Today's school libraries make essential contributions to the education of young people. In responsive, dynamic, and modern learning environments, libraries promote the development of skills and dispositions that align directly with existing priority areas for school leaders: Reading comprehension. STEM learning. Cross-disciplinary connections. Innovative, entrepreneurial thinking. Citizenship and social justice within the school and in the community. Local and global contexts for inquiry. Safe spaces for students. Differentiated, individualized support for diverse needs. Digital learning for students and teachers. Virtual, collaborative, and flexible learning spaces. Resourceful allocation and use of materials and time. Achievement of academic standards.

Your school library can amplify your school's progress toward these goals, through actions that you may never have considered as within the purview or potential of the library. School librarians are often forward-thinking and forward-acting leaders in their schools, and where libraries are well integrated into schools, they offer an unparalleled capacity to promote student learning. Libraries as key contributors in strengthening today's schools may challenge some antiquated notions, like the library as a hallowed, silent room for selecting and checking out books. Today's school libraries are a healthy bustle of conversation, where students use diverse tools for active learning. Many libraries have movable shelves and furniture to allow for collaboration and creativity. Gone are the big banks of desktop computers, replaced with charging stations and tablets. School librarians tend to be stereotyped as keepers of books and monitors of student behavior. There is some truth in this reputation, in that the best school librarians do have a deep knowledge of children's and young adult literature as well as expertise in listening to and interacting with young people. But in addition to their focus on literature and reading, today's librarians are trained to help students use a range of personal and school-issued devices to find and use information from an array of sources and platforms. Librarians do more than supervise students' information activities; they teach and model skills and dispositions for multiple literacies, and they design digital media and instructional materials according to student and curricular needs.

Still, with prominent misconceptions in media and mind-sets, it's clear why someone might ask if school libraries are still around or are worthwhile for today's kids. Even some school leaders may think they don't need libraries, because they have outdated ideas about what school libraries are. These impressions need some refocusing and refreshing to give a more accurate and relevant perspective on today's school libraries. As we tackle those outmoded assumptions, we'll see how a comprehensive, integrated library program contributes to successful learning.

Like schools in general, school libraries are a blend of established and newer philosophies, brand-new and make-do spaces, and unique attributes that represent the school community. School librarians specialize in two professional areas: library science and education. They draw upon this knowledge to implement a program designed to meet the needs of their particular schools, taking into account a range of factors, from the curriculum to the learning needs of the children. There is no singular set of circumstances that must be in place to make a library flourish, though a visit to several school libraries would reveal commonalities.

If you were to step into a school library, you would likely observe some of the processes and products that comprise school libraries' fundamental connection to schoolwide goals for student learning. You might see a librarian providing readers' advisory to help a child select a book for independent reading. In this instance, the librarian is simultaneously applying information about the child's interests, reading and language needs, and personal qualities (e.g., reading history, maturity, subject preferences, confidence, independence) to recommend books.

But many other teaching and learning interactions go on in today's school libraries. Students may be gathered around a table covered with open books, mobile devices, and notes, excitedly giving suggestions to solve a problem. This seemingly relaxed, casual scene echoes the collaborative work environments of innovative companies, where the tools and spaces encourage and promote sharing, access to a range of information resources and tools for productivity, and accountability within group processes. A librarian might be co-teaching with a classroom teacher, giving a mini-lesson on attribution of images before students search for photographs for a multimedia project. The teacher and librarian each draw upon their specialized expertise to guide students through the expectations for content and process, and students spend most of the class period searching for their photographs, with the librarian and teacher assisting individuals and small groups.

The library website, sometimes called the virtual library or library portal, gives students focused content to support reading and research as well as access to subscription-based resources and recommended apps and websites. In an activity like the image search just described, students might access the tools right in the physical library space. But with an effectively designed, well-equipped library website, students can also take the virtual voices of their librarian and teachers to scaffold their navigation of materials outside the library, supporting their learning at home or elsewhere. In chapter 7, I'll explain how librarians can work with technology administrators to design and maintain a web presence that grants students the best access and pathways for using library resources and other tools online.

The many online library "spaces" accommodate many uses and many users. Classroom teachers sign up for class library visits via online calendar. On the library blog, parents view students' multimedia products, such as interactive posters and digital stories. Community members view archived video of author visits conducted via video chat. Teachers compile bibliographies for curricular units using the library catalog. Students match reading needs and interests with the offerings of the library catalog. From students in kindergarten to grade 12, to teachers and staff, to parents, caregivers, and community members, the physical and virtual library extends space, opportunity, information, and guidance to the school. The librarians lead the way.

THE ROLES OF LIBRARIANS AND LIBRARIES

The core competencies of librarianship as described by the American Library Association are (1) foundations of the profession, (2) information resources, (3) organization of recorded knowledge and information, (4) technological knowledge and skills, (5) reference and user services, (6) research, (7) continuing education and lifelong learning, and (8) administration and management.[1] Beyond mastery of these core areas consistent across the profession, librarians have specialized knowledge for working in particular settings, like public, academic, or school libraries.

The specialized knowledge of school librarians enables them to fulfill five roles: teacher, instructional partner, information specialist, program administrator, and leader.[2] The following sections explain the tasks that comprise these roles. It is helpful to keep in mind that in practice, you may see a school librarian embody and balance these roles in different ways, depending on the circumstances and needs of the school environment. Variability in schedule, roles of other teaching faculty, and centralized versus localized school library purchasing may promote or limit the need and opportunity for the librarian to fulfill all five roles.

In looking at the five roles, you'll notice that the first two both refer to instruction: teacher and instructional partner. The latter still implies teaching, but involves a partnership with colleagues. Sometimes the partnership is a co-teaching scenario. For example, as a middle school librarian, I co-taught seventh-grade math students during monthly library visits. My math teacher colleague and I worked to find articles about the class's current math topic, and together, we facilitated students' reading and discussions about mathematics in careers and real-world applications. This example illustrates that being an instructional partner is not just about giving instruction, but also involves planning instruction, which encompasses advising on materials, resources, and instructional design.

Teacher

As a teacher, the librarian plans lessons, teaches and co-teaches, and assesses student learning. Although there are exceptions in some states and schools, this role is primarily one of professional teacher, rather than support staff. In fact, some people in the school library field prefer the title "teacher librarian" or "school library teacher" in order to emphasize the teacher part of the job. This distinction is of note to school leaders in matters of teacher evaluation, professional development, and contractual considerations, such as planning time.[3]

Whether or not the word "teacher" is part of your school librarian's title, this role is one of the most important factors in school librarians' potential impact on student learning. "Teacher" denotes the librarian's central role in providing instruction, and school leaders exert considerable influence on how (and whether) this teaching takes place. Schedule is a particularly key component in school librarians' capacity to teach. We'll examine types of schedules in chapter 7, and look at examples of school schedules that open up teaching time for librarians and students, as well as some circumstances that may restrict students' instructional time with librarians.

Instructional Partner

As instructional partners, librarians work with classroom teachers to plan instruction that may or may not happen in the library. In library-embedded lessons, students learn information, inquiry, reading, and research skills in a sequence that aligns with and complements the classroom curriculum. In lessons for which the librarian serves as more of a consultant or facilitator, librarians may guide teachers to useful applications or websites for students, suggest library materials, or facilitate small-group or individual students' information search processes in the library. They also refer teachers to professional resources and communities for networking and learning.

As instructional partners, librarians are trained to model creative, innovative approaches to inquiry. They demonstrate the capacity and pedagogy to foster students' persistence and curiosity in learning, even in a world of immediate answers and on-demand information. They help classroom teachers to inject students' content learning with information literacy. Because they see students year after year, even in a building with just three or four grade levels, librarians can uphold consistent expectations for students' research skills. Librarians attend to process in finding and using information, which bolsters efforts to shift students away from tendencies for speedy clicking, scrolling, and scanning without much active learning. School leaders can look to their librarians for practices that exemplify motivation for learning in today's information environments. When observing librarians as instructional partners, you will see professionals serving as collaborator, mentor, coach, and facilitator of student-centered learning.

Information Specialist

Librarians are your in-house information experts. Across educational and organizational settings, librarians model for students, patrons, and employees the navigation of information tools, the evaluation of information sources, and excitement for inquiry. They provide reference and reading guidance, and they also teach their users "how to fish" by introducing resources, strategies, and self-reflection in information-seeking processes so that users may learn to use these skills independently.

Turn to the library to support your school's efforts at cultivating students' deep learning and understanding. Inquiry-based, problem-based, and project-based learning thrive in the school library, because librarians connect information seeking and content creation. One of the most important contributions of your school librarian to teachers' and students' information skills is introducing them to content beyond the "free web." The free web is what most people know as the Internet, where free content is available to read, search, and use. But school librarians can open your students' and teachers' eyes to the "invisible web," the trove of resources that includes reference databases, which many libraries access through school or regional subscriptions. These sources are distinct from the free web for many reasons. First, the content is mostly unique—not everything is available on the Internet, after all—and includes books, maps, articles, images, videos, and audio, among other formats. In reference databases and other academically oriented resources, the information is vetted and selected for research purposes, and many databases are designed specifically for student use, with features to support students' reading, language, and learning needs. Further, the information is organized and searchable through various methods, which means that there are more ways to find content than the search box method that people predominantly use on the free web. Librarians know these sources, and they also know how to teach students and teachers effective use of search strategies like keywords, subject browsing, and source-specific tools, such as subject trees and graphic interfaces. Librarians can also guide students' use of enhanced features for using this content, such as bibliographic tools.

Richness of content across resources—print, online, free web, or invisible—introduces complications in access and evaluation: how to find things, through what channels at school and at home, and with what measure of equity for students across diverse living and socioeconomic settings. As information experts and teachers, school librarians lead and facilitate these processes not only for students, but for teachers and families as well.

The librarian and library resources complement and contribute to technology integration efforts from classroom teachers and technology specialists. If your school has a technology specialist, this person's role overlaps somewhat with, but remains distinct from, the roles of the librarian.[4] The technology specialist or coach has expertise in digital tools for differentiation, instruction, and assessment; strategies for advising, coaching, and providing professional development for teachers; pedagogy for utilizing technology in learning; and digital citizenship. They can provide visionary leadership as they work to foster "digital age environments" for teachers and students.[5] It is common for both the school librarian and the technology specialist to field requests from teachers for tech support and troubleshooting, computer supplies, or help setting up equipment. Depending on their assigned tasks (which may include this support), both librarians and technology specialists may address these needs.

In a school without a technology specialist, the librarian may assume that role within his or her other responsibilities. Your school is very fortunate if you have both of these professionals on the staff, as the combined areas of expertise of the librarian and technology specialist are a perfect match for technology in learning, including increasingly popular forms such as blended or hybrid learning (for example, flipped classrooms and MOOCs, or massive open online courses).

Program Administrator

This area is the management role for the school library. According to the American Association of School Librarians, "As program administrator, the [school librarian] ensures that all members of the learning community have access to resources that meet a variety of needs and interests."[6] In my experience, when most people consider what a librarian's job might entail, these are the tasks that come to mind, since many of them relate in some way to book borrowing. It's true that the program administrator role involves book circulation and collection development. However, the outsider's vantage point may not recognize the level of expertise and coordination that goes into this role. The complexity of program administration emerges when the various components are laid out, especially in the case of librarians working across multiple buildings.

The particulars may vary by school district, but typical to this role are managing and developing the collection, establishing relationships with book and database vendors, coordinating with state or regional consortia on license agreements for digital tools and databases, cataloging and processing books, and managing book circulation. In addition, there are both day-to-day tasks and more visionary, long-term work. This role encompasses schedule, library space, mission and strategic plan, communication about the library program, web presence and online tools, community partnerships, and library policies. Professional librarians are trained to coordinate these needs in the school with the appropriate personnel and follow the protocols for budgeting and spending funds, working with building operations, arranging for license agreements, and maintaining technology hardware and applications, including library catalog software and educational technology.

There are both professional and clerical dimensions to these responsibilities, and it's highly beneficial to have aides or volunteers to support such tasks as reshelving returned books and processing new magazines. Although circumstances exist where nonprofessional employees or volunteers staff a library, this is not a best practice. The important, but still clerical tasks should be the extent of their contributions. The professional hand in the administration of the program enables the library to function as effectively as possible within the school infrastructure, by operationalizing the mission and priorities of the school through specific and aligned services, resources, and instruction. To this end, in upcoming chapters I address not only library-embedded teaching and learning aspects of the school library, but also operational-level considerations (e.g., schedules, procedures, budgets, materials, and staffing) that allow school librarians to do their best work for students.

Leader

The last of the five school librarian roles is leader. This is the role that brings together the other roles to produce visible outcomes for students, teachers, and school communities. As leaders, librarians promote and implement a range of library services to students and teachers. A library program can't be quiet in the school, and though librarians can choose how they lead, they can't choose not to lead.

In the leadership role, it is an ongoing practice for school librarians to look outward to the needs of the school, then reflexively back to the library program to consider what it can offer in terms of resources, instruction, and ideas, and then back out to the school to monitor and adjust. The library curriculum has clear objectives for student learning, but its implementation is most relevant in combination with classroom teachers' instruction. Thus, librarians must proactively seek collaborations with teachers, know the scope and sequence of schoolwide curricula, and align resources with subject-area content. With all of this information and perspective, librarians develop and provide opportunities for students to practice and master a range of inquiry, reading, and thinking skills. This is the work of an educational leader. This is the work of a person who has a big-picture view. This is a person whose skill set and vision are needed by the school.

A glimpse into my philosophy of training school librarians is helpful in understanding this leadership role. As an educator of school librarians, I aim to cultivate this leadership "package" in the current and preservice librarians who take my courses. In practice, leadership is a capacity composed of a blend of skills and dispositions, and the school library candidates prepare for this role almost continuously. This process is less about learning explicit skills in "executing leadership" than identifying and acting upon two critical things. First is context: How does the library program fit into the students' and teachers' needs at a given time, and long term? Second is opportunity: How can the librarian attend to and grasp opportunities to fulfill those needs? The school library candidates practice this equation of context and opportunity through competency-based projects. For instance, when they write a collaborative unit plan, they do this with the understanding that they wouldn't teach the unit alone in the school setting. They would need collaborative partners, since the potential to collaborate doesn't usually just fall into one's lap. Essential to initiating collaboration are leadership actions, starting with reaching out to colleagues and explaining the learning outcomes made possible with library integration. In class, we discuss varying forms of successful collaborations, and how to plan, teach, and assess alongside classroom teachers. The process of designing instruction and selecting resources—that is, the actual unit and lesson plans—is only part of the big picture of implementing the unit with students and teachers. The leadership piece is essential in making library learning most impactful. Through leadership, school librarians form partnerships and deliver outcomes across stakeholder groups. They listen to and look for schoolwide needs, and bring together the people and resources to understand and serve those needs.

BRIDGES TO SCHOOL PRIORITIES

To carry out the five roles just summarized, school librarians follow the recommended policies and practices of the national professional organization of school librarians, the American Association of School Librarians (AASL, a division of the American Library Association). AASL offers nine Common Beliefs that are the foundation for the profession's standards, known as the Standards for the 21st-Century Learner. The beliefs are as follows:

- Reading is a window to the world.
- Inquiry provides a framework for learning.
- Ethical behavior in the use of information must be taught.
- Technology skills are crucial for future employment needs.
- Equitable access is a key component for education.
- The definition of information literacy has become more complex as resources and technologies have changed.
- The continuing expansion of information demands that all individuals acquire the thinking skills that will enable them to learn on their own.
- Learning has a social context.
- School libraries are essential to the development of learning skills.[7]

As teachers, instructional partners, information specialists, program administrators, and leaders, school librarians put these beliefs into action. These beliefs motivate the work of librarians and distinguish librarians from classroom teachers, technology specialists, and other educators in the school. Here are a few examples of these beliefs at work.

"Reading is a window to the world" can be seen in the many ways librarians promote reading across formats and purposes, from primary grade levels through high school. They model and scaffold reading opportunities for students' recreation, research, and personal informational needs. Librarians get to know students' interests, preferences, and abilities in reading. They apply their expert knowledge of children's and young adult resources to enable students to navigate through a carefully developed library collection that supports and inspires reading development and knowledge growth. See the sidebar "Collection Development" for more about how librarians equip libraries with the appropriate materials for student learning.

As proponents of students' right to read and promoters of intellectual freedom, librarians provide students choice and agency in selecting

Collection Development

The success of student learning in the library depends in large part on the librarian's careful maintenance, updating, and use of the collection with students and teachers. A collection that reflects diverse cultures, voices, and formats is a necessity today, yet can be a sizable challenge to manage under a tight budget.

School librarians aim to build a collection of reading materials and information resources that support students' needs as they pertain to the academic context (i.e., school-imposed research topics, reading choices, and curricular materials), personal information needs (such as resources on health, relationships, or consumer topics), and recreational reading (that is, reading and media for fun and personal interests). School librarians work hard to "maintain the collection," as they call it, meaning that they use professional selection sources to select materials that correspond to all of these needs at reading and interest levels suitable for the students. They weed or "deselect" books according to policies and guidelines of the school and the profession. They organize the shelving and books for access, possibly including cataloging, labeling, and signage. They perform actual maintenance on the books, repairing damage and wear. The shelves, the circulation desk, the class schedule, even the entry and exits to the school library are typically designed to accommodate book borrowing.

Ordering, circulating, maintaining, and recommending books are only part of the story of the library and reading, and only one way to tap the potential of the library. Thoughtful integration of library resources into student learning is also important, and wide, curriculum-aligned use of the library collection substantiates the expense of keeping the collection robust and current. This is a primary reason that professional librarians (not aides or volunteers) lead the best school libraries today, constantly and expertly weaving together instruction, access, and the collection.

reading materials so that students may expand their perspectives. They not only encourage students to become thoughtful and curious readers today; they also place confidence and value in the processes that create lifelong readers, such that students are motivated to pursue reading outside of school and beyond their K–12 experiences.

Another Common Belief is that "learning has a social context." School library spaces foster collaborative learning, conversation, and sharing of ideas, technology, and stories. Today's school library spaces reflect the social atmosphere of many current professional workplaces, where creativity and productivity happen not in isolation, but across big tables, around whiteboards or big screens, and within reach of wireless networks to support mobile devices—where online, another layer of social learning unfolds. Another aspect of social learning in the library is that as teaching partners, the librarian and classroom teachers model real-world collaborations for students. By nature of their respective backgrounds, they also design multidimensional learning experiences that blend information, digital, and civic literacies (among others) and content-area learning. Placing learning in authentic contexts is a key to inquiry, and part of that context is that learners are typically learning among others, whether they are in face-to-face settings or virtual spaces. Libraries embrace and support this aspect of learning.

A look at one last Common Belief will help acquaint you with the school library view of learning today: "The definition of information literacy has become more complex as resources and technologies have changed." Librarians model "multiple literacies" or "transliteracy" for students and teachers, helping students learn skills to find, use, and create content across diverse platforms. They encourage and guide students and teachers to find the best resources for information, such as the reference databases mentioned previously. They teach strategies for evaluating and sorting through diverse types of information. Librarians also instruct students to participate productively in social learning networks and to use a variety of devices and tools for accessing information, organizing sources, and producing writing, artwork, media, and other learning artifacts. Personalized learning, blended learning, and other individualized pathways are also connected to multiple literacies. Information and communication technology unchain teachers from lockstep processes and materials that students must use to learn a particular area of knowledge or skill. Given their roles of teacher and information specialist, librarians are in the position to teach the multiple literacies needed for successful access to and use of resources.

To help illustrate the relationship between the library program and the school as a whole, I have worked from these Common Beliefs to suggest three conceptual "bridges." These bridges establish the big picture of purposeful, well-supported school library integration as a significant, distinct contributor to school priorities. I grouped the Common Beliefs into three sets and aligned them with the bridges. In the chapters that follow, I will drill down into the particulars of that big picture with examples. Here are the three bridges.

BRIDGE 1 *Libraries provide links across content areas to support interdisciplinary learning.*

These three AASL Common Beliefs are most relevant to this conceptual bridge:

- Reading is a window to the world.
- Inquiry provides a framework for learning.
- School libraries are essential to the development of learning skills.

Library-integrated learning draws connections between information skills and subject-area content. For instance, as American history students study primary source documents, they are building both social studies content knowledge and library and information skills. School librarians collaborating to teach with social studies teachers make these connections most explicit. Their collaborative lessons model skills that include integrating prior classroom learning and background knowledge; reading for bias and social and cultural context; organizing and self-monitoring reading; identifying themes and keywords for note taking; self-assessing learning; and seeking help when needed.[8]

Practicing information skills in context within subject areas and not in isolation is one potential outcome of library-integrated learning. Another is the interdisciplinary learning afforded by inquiry. The study of epidemic disease, for example, integrates health, science, human geography, mathematics, policy and government, and reading/writing/listening/speaking. This fundamental bridge across content areas is one that the librarian can strengthen by leading collaborations with classroom teachers across subject areas.

BRIDGE 2 *Libraries foster transliteracy skills across information sources and tasks.*

These AASL Common Beliefs are pertinent to this conceptual bridge:

- Technology skills are crucial for future employment needs.
- The definition of information literacy has become more complex as resources and technologies have changed.
- The continuing expansion of information demands that all individuals acquire the thinking skills that will enable them to learn on their own.

I mentioned transliteracy above in the context of multiple literacies, which reflect a growing list of competencies for reading and interacting with texts, media, and people. The idea of teaching multiple literacies represents a relatively recent shift in how the school library profession refers to its purview of standards and skills. "Information literacy" is the term that describes proficiency in information-related skills—that is, identifying an information need, locating and evaluating information, and using that information effectively.[9] Introducing multiple "literacies" doesn't diminish the importance of information literacy or school librarians' focus on teaching it. But with the introduction of the most recent school library standards (the 2007 *Standards for the 21st-Century Learner*), information literacy is taught along with other skills, including technology or digital literacy, media literacy, and visual literacy.

What students gain from a library program that serves as a consistent, visible link between multiple literacies and content areas is the instruction of transliteracy. Transliteracy encompasses multiple literacies (e.g., reading, viewing, and interacting or engaging with content across formats and topics), and most importantly, it covers skills needed to shift across (hence, the prefix "trans-") these modes of attending to information. In teaching transliteracy, school librarians "guide students and teachers to formats most appropriate to the learning task," "provide instruction specific to searching for information in various formats," and "promote critical thinking by connecting learners with the world of information in multiple formats."[10] Thus, one objective of transliteracy is navigating information landscapes and demonstrating appropriate literacies. Another outcome of transliteracy is taking those literacies from one learning experience and applying them to another context, class, or project. Library-integrated instruction exhibits this transfer by design and principle, and librarians call it out directly in their teaching, as in this brief scenario of a librarian introducing a lesson to an eleventh-grade American history class:

> Remember when we read those two articles about fracking in science class last month, and you figured out the authors' points of view? What were some of the strategies you used to do that? Yes—you considered the sources—one was a website from an oil and gas company, and the other was a letter to the editor from a wildlife organization. You researched and thought about the authority and bias of the writers, and the target audiences for that information.

> Today in social studies class, you are going to apply many of those same strategies. You will be reading a newspaper article and a pamphlet, both written about 150 years ago on the topic of post–Civil War Reconstruction. The first time you read through these, get yourself ready for note taking by focusing on that author perspective again. With that in mind, what will you look for first as you read?

Embedding library experiences into the curriculum provides transliteracy skills students need to thrive in today's technology-, media-, and information-focused environment. In this way, the library program supports college and career readiness skills.

BRIDGE 3 *Libraries build collaborative, accountable communities of learners.*

The following AASL Common Beliefs shape this last conceptual bridge between the library program and student learning across school programs:

- Equitable access is a key component for education.
- Ethical behavior in the use of information must be taught.
- Learning has a social context.

School libraries (and libraries in general) offer access and opportunity for individual learning pursuits, community experiences, and social interactions. Equity and access are priorities for all libraries, especially libraries in K–12 schools, where equity and access relate to making appropriate library materials and spaces available within the physical library and through the virtual library online. In the program administrator role, the school librarian selects and provides curriculum-aligned materials in formats that meet the range of student needs in the school, including reading levels, cognitive abilities, language, and special needs such as visual or hearing impairments. In the leader role, the school librarian works to make the school community—which includes students and families accessing resources from home—aware of library materials for their use.

Access also pertains to use of the physical library, and school librarians depend on their school leaders to help facilitate access to the library during classes and also for individual visits before or after school, or during lunch. The issue of access to the physical library space segues into the school library as a social learning community, wherein school libraries parallel many professional work settings in their support of individual and collaborative processes. Librarians purposefully integrate the teaching of social responsibility, civility, and respect for other people and perspectives. School-age children are developing identities as citizens, learners, and thinkers, and libraries foster both independence and social awareness to support this growth. The library's social community is both face-to-face and virtual, setting up a notable example of how the library stands apart from other classes and instruction in the school. Library-integrated learning features a lot of technology, including online databases, content creation and curation, search tools, collaborative applications, social media sharing, and more. Today's libraries are becoming synonymous with technology-driven experiences.

Yet, the use of technology in education isn't reserved for library learning, and this book's emphasis on technology use in the library isn't intended to detract from other teachers' and programs' instructional technology initiatives. What school leaders need to know about the library's approach to educational technology is that the instruction incorporates content long taught by school librarians, including ethical use of information. That subject takes on new meaning with today's technology, but the core principles remain: Attribute information sources appropriately and accurately. Respect intellectual property. Be truthful in representing an author's ideas. Honor privacy in information. Don't present someone else's work as your own. Disclose information only for its intended audience. Don't plagiarize. Across subject areas (bridge 1), across literacies (bridge 2), library instruction teaches students to be ethical users of information with peers, with teachers, and in communities of all kinds (bridge 3).

Throughout this book, I will refer to these bridges to illustrate how school librarians use their five roles, building from the foundation of the Common Beliefs, to help students become strong and independent readers, creative thinkers, and lifelong learners. School libraries can reach their potential with the support, partnership, and ideas of school leaders. Today's school principals, curriculum directors, and other educational leaders work in climates of high-stakes, highly visible accountability. This probably describes you, if you're reading this book. You know well the expectations you face, often under stretched budgets, to produce improved academic results from diverse populations of learners. I believe that you want the outcomes of the bridges between the school and the library program. To get there, school leaders should uphold high expectations for their school library programs.

EXPECTATIONS FOR THE SCHOOL LIBRARY

In talking to school librarians at conferences, hearing what practicing librarians report in my graduate courses, and browsing school library discussion forums and listservs, two perspectives on school principals stand out. First are the principals librarians describe as fantastic and supportive. "I love my principal!" these librarians exclaim. Sometimes they offer the ultimate compliment: "She (or he) really gets it." A principal who "gets it" recognizes that the library isn't a study hall, babysitting center, or computer lab. This principal views the library as a strong contributor to student learning in the school, and his or her support enables the librarian to carry out the five roles that in turn produce student achievement. This "fantastic" principal has high expectations for the school library.

On the other hand, a different and equally memorable category of school principal tends to crop up in discussions with school librarians.

Sometimes with a shrug, and sometimes with an air of frustration, librarians in this group report that their principals "just don't understand what I do." These might be principals who pull the librarian to cover classes for absent teachers. They might close the library at arrival or dismissal time to have the librarian serve bus duty, or they don't grant budget requests for the library because "there are lots of books already." Principals in this group—generally speaking—demonstrate lower expectations for the librarian as a teacher when they disrupt the librarian's scheduled lessons with students. They show minimal expectations for the library's role in independent reading by having librarians close the door for bus duty, thus preventing students from borrowing books and getting readers' advisory (professional book selection guidance) from the librarian. "Lots of books" on the shelf is not necessarily indicative of a collection effectively aligned to the curriculum, with current materials.

The principal who "doesn't get it" isn't clueless, and these librarians aren't harboring ill will toward their school leaders. They just know that administrator-level decisions, like teacher coverage, bus duty, and budget, determine how effectively the library can serve students. When library programs aren't integrated purposefully into the learning environment of the school, their benefits for student learning aren't likely to be fully realized. Like any other department, a school library program with less perceived or measured value risks reduction or entire cuts in staffing and materials. Retiring librarians may not be replaced, or librarians may be reassigned to classroom positions when teacher positions are vacant. These decisions aren't likely made hastily or painlessly, but they may not be made with the full picture of what a library can offer. Principals who "don't get it" definitely do get that they are facing immense pressure, limited budgets, and an array of diverse student and family needs. They just may never have seen or learned about the powerful impact that a library program can have on student learning, so they don't know the level at which they can set their expectations.

School leaders should expect the library and librarian to teach and assess standards-aligned curricula, with materials selected carefully and technology incorporated purposefully. Librarians should model technology use that tends toward the invisible and natural; that is, technology-integrated learning that isn't a "special occasion," but a seamless choice to use (or not use) technology when it fits (or doesn't fit) the task or an individual learner's needs.[11] At the level of the teachers and staff, your library program should lead a reflective culture of teaching and ongoing professional growth. School librarians expect these outcomes for a library program, and school leaders should, too.

DISCUSSING SCHOOL LIBRARY IMPACT

Can best practices in one educational program really make a difference across the array of initiatives and issues that schools are trying to address? The body of research known as "school library impact studies" demonstrates how the role of school libraries aligns with priorities of school leaders. In more than sixty studies conducted in twenty-three states, quality school library programs are shown to be a factor in increases in student achievement.[12] Many core concerns in leading a school—organization and administration of space, resources, staff, and scheduling—are likewise the basis for leading and managing quality library programs. To be clear, the school library impact studies are largely correlational in methodology, not causal. Yet, correlational research provides compelling links between quality school library programs and student learning, particularly when studies across states and settings show similar outcomes.[13]

Two publications that summarize and make accessible the school library impact studies are *School Library Research Summarized* and "School Library Impact Studies: Research Summary."[14] Library program components are discussed by category with corresponding state studies in "The Research Says," a chapter by school library educator and researcher

Audrey Church in *Leverage Your Library Program to Raise Test Scores*.[15] These publications identify similar components of school library programs found to have a positive association with student achievement. I will list the areas briefly here, and discuss them in context throughout the book. For additional information on the research studies, please see the publications named for source listings and discussion. *School Library Research Summarized* provides a particularly efficient and comprehensive chart of program components and corresponding studies by state.

Several salient, common factors of quality school library programs are associated with student learning. A full-time professional librarian with support staff is a major factor, as is the librarian's collaboration with teachers and principals. The library collection and student access to the library and the materials both within and outside the library are also important. The librarian as a teacher of information literacy and leader of technology integration within the school curriculum is another contributing component to student learning; note that these teaching and leadership roles line up with the identified roles for school librarians. Summer reading programs and reading incentive programs are common features of quality school library programs. Professional development provided by the librarian to teachers is another factor. Finally, in several studies, larger library expenditures per student show a relationship with higher test scores.[16]

A particularly noteworthy finding across several studies relates to the narrowing of the achievement gap, a prominent concern of school leaders, policy makers, and communities. The most recent Colorado school library study "suggests that effective school libraries can be of even greater help to students who are struggling most than to those already performing at grade level or better." The study also found "stronger library programs were also associated with reduced percentages of students receiving unsatisfactory CSAP [state test] scores, thereby helping to close the achievement gap."[17]

As Hartzell describes, studies that control for demographic differences and subgroups represent an important advancement in school library studies in the last twenty-five years. (Pre-1990s, library studies didn't typically account for these differences.)[18] For example, the 2011 statewide school library study conducted in Pennsylvania showed that for "student groups that tend to experience achievement gaps—economically disadvantaged, Hispanic, Black, and those with IEPs (Individualized Education Programs)—Reading and Writing results are markedly better when those students attend a school with a librarian with library support staff." Further, students in these subgroups "benefit[ted] more proportionally than the general school population."[19]

Many aspects of quality school library programs, especially scheduling and budget allocation, operate under varying levels of influence of the school principal and district administration, as Hartzell notes in "The Multiple Dimensions of Principal Involvement." However, influence isn't represented by dollars alone: "As important as money is in library operation, it is not the only measure of principal support. Equally important is the role the principal plays in creating a school environment that values and promotes student library use and adult interaction with the librarian."[20]

In this book, I will describe specific steps principals can take to create that environment. One factor is a library tightly connected to and driven by the school mission and culture. As library science researcher and educator Carol Gordon writes, "A 21st century learning environment challenges the restrictions of time and place that characterize traditional schooling and opens opportunities for school library practices to transcend the walls of the library, contributing in a broader context of school reform."[21] The competencies and dispositions that enable these outcomes are embedded in nearly everything that librarians, teachers, and school leaders do. These topics are woven throughout this book just as they are woven into the work of a school leader. Following is a preview of these topics by chapter.

CHAPTER OVERVIEW

Chapter 2: Makerspaces and Learning Commons

Student-centered learning is the focus of chapter 2. School libraries are hubs of innovative learning and teaching, including the settings known as makerspaces and the learning commons model. This chapter offers examples of learning experiences in learning commons and makerspaces across grade levels and subject areas. Strategies are suggested for school leaders to communicate and support the potential for library spaces to foster student-centered learning. Keeping in mind that the school library provides resources for students' independent use outside the library walls, this chapter also presents opportunities for maximizing the library's resources for your school's blended learning initiatives, such as flipped instruction.

Chapter 3: Reading Across the Curriculum

Reading is often considered the most characteristic aspect of school library programs, and chapter 3 explores that role in the context of efforts to develop a schoolwide culture of reading and multiple literacies. The Common Core State Standards (CCSS) place a strong emphasis on the reading of complex texts, particularly informational texts, and you may be addressing this shift with your teachers now. In this process, you may be finding it challenging to build time in the school schedule for thoughtful reading and comprehension of complex texts. The school librarian is in a unique position to pull together reading skills across subject areas through collaboration with teachers. While classroom teachers lead in their respective areas of content instruction, librarians take the lead in guiding students as they encounter texts that cross formats and ways of reading. This chapter provides examples of how a school library program's resources and lessons support reading instruction and cultivate a culture of reading.

Chapter 4: Inquiry and Critical Thinking

This chapter addresses the construction of rich, layered questions for inquiry by teachers and students, building on the student-centered learning opportunities introduced in chapter 2. I wouldn't be alone if I were to argue that an ultimate goal of education is to teach students how to learn. Teachers and librarians must enable students to transfer understandings and think critically, and to take ownership of their learning in school settings and beyond.

Through a schoolwide commitment to inquiry-based research projects, assignments that build deep understanding, and the processes of building and responding to essential questions, students can develop thoughtful, productive approaches to inquiry learning. With the help of invested school leaders, the school librarian can assume a significant role in helping teachers to design inquiry-based learning experiences, or curate resources to support inquiry. The chapter provides an introduction to information search and research models, which you may consider adopting across your school or system to build a consistent and cumulative approach to inquiry for students as they progress through their education.

Chapter 5: Assessment for Learning

It may be surprising for teachers and school leaders to hear that assessment is an ongoing and important professional development topic for school librarians. Chapter 5 expands assessment beyond the calculation of report card grades or numerical points for assignments, and into assessment strategies that inform teaching and cultivate students' self-assessment skills. The school library affords opportunities to study progress at the school level on a longitudinal basis, and we will also examine this form of assessment.

Chapter 6: Responding to Diverse Needs

The school library is a valuable asset for building positive relationships across the school, with students' families, and with the broader community. The library is a lifeline for students' at-home learning through reference databases, learning tools, and virtual library services, where the "voice" of the school librarian in curated collections and resources scaffolds students' independent learning. Through its collection, the school library also offers information and stories to build connections to students' families, languages, and cultural diversity. With library parent volunteer programs, parent and family school resources, and programs for families and the community, school leaders can shape families' positive experiences with the school and support student success, as well as demonstrate the value and roles of the school library at the local level.

Chapter 7: Practical Matters

This chapter offers ideas for putting in place the spaces, people, and opportunities that allow student learning to thrive through the school library program. I suggest some initial, manageable steps for revitalizing the school library. I also describe some school policies and practices that can enable and occasionally constrain innovative school library practices. From my own experiences as well as those school librarians have shared with me, I present some common dilemmas facing school leaders and school librarians, and consider possible solutions.

Chapter 8: Excellence for Libraries, Excellence for Schools

The final chapter offers a reflection on the relationship between school leaders' instructional and organizational goals and a dynamic school library. In this chapter we revisit the bridges between a robust school library program and action areas of school leaders.

LIBRARY INTEGRATION IN THE SCHOOL

Chapters 2 through 6 open with vignettes involving school librarians and other educators, working together to investigate topics with schoolwide ramifications, such as integrating new forms of assessment into traditional school projects. By placing the library in the context of the school and community, not just within stories about "library issues," I hope to suggest scenarios that inspire you to picture your school reaping the benefits of a library that plays a more central role in student learning.

The school environment is a place where successes and failures matter not just within the walls of the building, but also outside, in the community and beyond. Education is everybody's business, and it's a complicated business for certain. "Running a good school is no simple matter," write Bernie Trilling and Charles Fadel. "A number of complex relationships and supporting systems must all work together to bring the best possible learning experience to each and every child."[22]

Even the most capable and well-intentioned school librarian cannot alone orchestrate the library's position in the school. School libraries clearly need the support and trust of school leaders in order to function successfully for students. This support serves the best interests of the students and the administrators themselves, as the same outcomes that school libraries can generate are the attributes assessed in principals' competencies and evaluation standards. These include implementing an aligned and rigorous curriculum, responding to diverse needs of students and families, and achieving high levels of academic success.[23]

GETTING STARTED

Your school library program and school librarian hold great potential for learning and sources of leadership. The school librarian has specific expertise that can inform decisions, ideas, and actions that propel the entire school. You are probably reading this book because you're interested in the idea of reimagining school libraries, a process with potential to institute significant results for student learning. The librarian's role is part of what must be reimagined.

This vision of school libraries as tightly woven into the priorities of the school may not sound like where your school library is right now,

Sorting Out Library Job Titles

In this book, I use the title "school librarian" to identify the professional who teaches library classes and embedded library instruction and manages the library program. In 2010, the American Association of School Librarians officially adopted "school librarian" as a "title for its professionals that is clear to other educators, administrators, and the public, and that presents a common nomenclature for all publications and advocacy efforts."[24] I agree with this choice and its rationale. The name "school librarian" is classic and clear, and there is less potential for confusion with other roles in schools, like instructional technology specialists or staff responsible for technology equipment. "Librarian" also recognizes the professional training within the discipline of library and information science.

However, other titles are still in use. In keeping with the state teaching licensure or certification, the job title is typically standard within the districts in the same state, though not always. When I taught in Pennsylvania, teachers and students knew me as the school librarian, but my listing in the faculty directory referred to me as the "library science teacher." You might be familiar with other versions of the school librarian job title and its acronyms: school library teacher, teacher librarian, library media specialist (sometimes abbreviated as LMS, MS, or even "media spec"), media coordinator, and various other combinations. One school I visited in Philadelphia several years ago even had a "cybrarian." For me, titles like "media coordinator" and "cybrarian" evoke too specific a time period and can sound outdated very quickly.

As outlined in chapter 1, AASL describes five official roles of this job, regardless of the chosen title: teacher, instructional partner, information specialist, program administrator, and leader.[25]

and that's OK. Whether your school has a strong program, a program you don't know much about, or no library at all, this book will provide the rationale, questions to ask, and exemplars to follow in supporting the best library for your students. See the appendix for a checklist to help you connect what you read here with the library at your school. If you're wondering about the job title used for your school librarian, see the previous sidebar "Sorting Out Library Job Titles" for some background on this topic.

I'll also acknowledge some tough questions that you may be asking about the arguments presented in the book. For instance: How can the librarian provide leadership in teaching the Common Core State Standards when our school is just in its initial years of implementation and assessment? What do students need the library to provide, considering all they can find online? What does the school librarian provide that is different from what other educators do?

You might want to know how your school can support a budget for a librarian when facing cuts to classroom teachers. Or, even if the librarian's position is fairly secure, you might wonder how far a small-budget or no-budget library can go toward becoming such a big part of the school. In upcoming chapters, I'll suggest some strategies, solutions, and ideas to address these questions. By reshaping the school library's role plan for shared and strategic leadership, you will be better equipped to pursue and attain your schoolwide goals, including high expectations for student learning, meaningful family and community engagement, and reflective, ongoing professional development. Read on to find out what active support of your library can do for your students. When you see how the library can become an essential element of a vibrant and successful school, you just might be the next person to answer whether students still need a library with, "Absolutely! Let me tell you why."

CHAPTER 2

Makerspaces and Learning Commons

Supporting Student-Centered Learning

Service Learning in the Library Makerspace

Sean is the school librarian at a high school where the ninth graders complete a yearly spring service learning project. These projects reflect topics of personal significance to the students, and the teachers have been really pleased with student choices and learning experiences the last few years. The building administrators often refer to this project as an exemplar of student-centered learning. Recent student projects have included a public service announcement about reducing water bottle waste in the cafeteria, an oral history event at a local assisted living facility, and the construction and installation of a rainwater collection system to water the schoolyard habitat. Traditionally, the project follows a process whereby students gather background information on their ideas and build proposals with their English language arts (ELA) teachers, who serve as the project facilitators. Students complete the projects alongside community leaders and subject experts, and then write self-reflections at the end.

Although the background research and reflection are required components, the depth of research and the project development processes vary across the ninth-grade ELA classes. In recent years, a growing number of students have utilized technology and design tools to research and carry out their projects, which has led to new kinds of endeavors, such as digital storytelling with the residents at the assisted living facility and the use of social media to acquire donations of materials to sew pet blankets for an animal shelter.[1] Students are sharing their projects with the community and the world in more ways every year, through videos, blogs, and social media.

Some of the ninth-grade ELA teachers play a supervisory role in the project, having students work mostly outside of class, and letting them use technology if they want to try it or know how already. Other teachers are more explicit in encouraging and facilitating the use of technology. And last year, a few teachers took students to the library's new "makerspace" for their projects.

The library makerspace was once a library workroom. With approval from the principal and some assistance from the district's technology coordinator and operations department, this reconceived space now has a basic 3D printer, two sewing machines, sliding whiteboards on the wall, and sundry bins and trays of electronic equipment and art supplies. Most of the tables move with casters. There is a centralized "juice bar," a hub of power cords for charging various mobile devices.

Awareness of the space is still building slowly across the faculty, and as school librarian, Sean is ready for a chance to introduce the makerspace as part of a more focused learning opportunity that is still independent and student-centered. This service learning project fits the bill perfectly. The ninth-grade principal, Marielena, is eager to promote the makerspace, so she has asked Sean to prepare a five-minute overview for the upcoming grade-level meeting, after which the teachers will share ideas and questions about using the new makerspace for a project with which many teachers are fairly pleased in its current state.

Here are Sean's talking points, aimed at addressing three common questions and concerns:

1. What is the "makerspace" in our school library?
2. How can our ninth graders use the makerspace for the service project?
3. What if I don't know enough about the tools that the kids want to use?

Sean and Marielena planned this last question together, as they anticipate some concern from teachers who aren't comfortable with projects going in multiple directions, or don't want to introduce complications or the need for troubleshooting. However, Sean and Marielena are confident that the students' motivation and engagement will be well worth some risk taking on the part of the teachers.

STUDENT-CENTERED LEARNING IN LIBRARY MAKERSPACES

In this chapter, we'll look at two recent innovations in configuring libraries—makerspaces and learning commons—as well as ways that libraries can support student-centered classroom pedagogies such as flipped classrooms and badging. I'll revisit Sean's talking points to organize this section. But first, what is a "makerspace"?

Makerspaces, hackerspaces, fab labs, and similarly titled spaces are a growing phenomenon, originating in community centers, churches, and public libraries, and now finding popularity and a home in school libraries. According to Makerspace.com, "Makerspaces represent the democratization of design, engineering, fabrication and education."[2] Makerspaces are a junction of space, materials, and supportive opportunity—a perfect fit for the mission of libraries, where people go for equitable access to materials and willing assistance in learning, information, and creative endeavors.

The physical spaces are sometimes repurposed offices and workrooms, with equipment and materials for making things, just as the name suggests. Makerspace products vary widely and may include robotics, machines, clothing, multimedia productions, musical compositions, and items like models, hardware, and tools and toys produced via 3D printer. Before the rise of the makerspace name, art and music rooms, computer and robotics labs, and home economics classrooms offered aspects of the makerspace philosophy over many decades. But the allocation of tools, equipment, and rooms in schools specifically for this idea called a "makerspace" is a relatively fresh movement. Like other makerspaces, the one at Sean and Marielena's school offers an intuitive and visible relationship between library resources and space for experimentation, design, and creativity.

In *Creating Innovators: The Making of Young People Who Will Change the World*, educator and author Tony Wagner highlights why authentic, problem-solving learning—like that afforded by makerspaces—is so critical for today's students: "Increasingly in the twenty-first century, what you know is far less important than what you can do with what you know. The interest in and the ability to create new knowledge to solve new problems is the single most important skill that all students must master today."[3]

Makerspaces, along with the learning commons and blended learning experiences that will be discussed in this chapter, provide forums for students to see what they can do with what they know, to adapt Wagner's language. Whether integrated into subject-area content or provided as a space for independent exploration, makerspaces give students choice, context for problem solving and inquiry, and space, both physical and conceptual. Granting choices in projects and processes illustrates both student-centered learning and the makerspace philosophy.

Interdisciplinary instruction in the library and makerspace represents a new vision of vocational and career learning. From the *Makerspace Playbook: School Edition*:

> Makerspaces borrow somewhat from the tradition of career technical education or vocational education, but they diverge by metaphorically, sometimes literally, tearing down the walls between the silos of classes in woodshop, computer science, home economics, automotive repair, etc. in pursuit of a more interdisciplinary goal. Makerspaces also recognize that making enriches the educational experience of students who are motivated to different extent in school.[4]

Makerspaces are especially well suited to STEM (science, technology, engineering, and math) projects. Although STEM learning isn't the only curriculum area appropriate for the makerspace, it is definitely a big focus. In writing about the role of school libraries in STEM education and the development of young people's identities as STEM learners, Subramaniam et al. propose that school libraries have different opportunities than formal classrooms in terms of innovative spaces and contexts for learning. Generating curiosity about science content in print and nonprint resources is one key component of the potential for STEM integration in the library. The "infus[ion] of technology and new media into the STEM learning process," led by librarians adept in digital tools, is another.[5]

With the makerspace philosophy in mind, let's examine Sean's next talking point: what the ninth graders can do with the makerspace for their service learning project. Some of the ELA teachers have already agreed to collaborate with Sean, so he starts his explanation with their roles. Following the traditional project development, the teachers will prepare students to write their proposals, then teach and assess the writing process. In a written composition, students will identify a need for service, pose a contributing voice or solution, and lay out a plan for a project.

Here is where Sean steps in as the librarian, functioning in his roles as teacher, instructional partner, and information specialist. Sean will strengthen the research process by guiding students through information seeking and use. He will ask students about their interests and point them to resources like videos, blogs, books, articles, and social media networks. Sean will model possible uses of the makerspace and invite students to explore them. For instance, students might sketch out ideas on the whiteboard, experiment with media production techniques (e.g., videos, digital art, or mapping), or practice fabric manipulation and sewing.

As they test ideas and materials in the makerspace, Sean will teach students to use their transliteracy skills to access and engage with diverse sources, and think deeply about their topics as they do so. Building on information literacy instruction over the course of the year, Sean will prompt them to evaluate sources for their needs and self-assess their processes. He will model the steps for students to access content in the formats they prefer, and teach them to curate collections of their work through digital tools that present a hyperlinked, visual, and interactive list of their information.

Once students are ready to make their projects, Sean will draw upon his relationships with other teachers in the school to bring them into the projects, according to their specialized expertise. By managing multiple student projects, varied groupings of learners and teachers, and activities, Sean exemplifies conceptual bridge 3 introduced in chapter 1: libraries build collaborative, accountable communities of learners. Learning is socially constructed, yet individual paths for learning flourish. Because Sean knows teachers and curriculum across grade levels in the school, he is a good point person to identify potential collaborators and invite their contributions to student work in the makerspace.

This leadership and collaborative strategy addresses Sean's third point to the teachers, in which he answers the potential question, "What if I don't know enough about the tools the kids want to use?"

Sean wants the teachers to understand that they are not expected to know everything about every project idea or tool that students may introduce. Part of the makerspace philosophy is that it is a fluid system of novices and experts working together to solve problems and learn. Not having all the answers can be unsettling for educators, but embracing the idea that knowledge comes from many places and people is a very current and essential perspective to model for children.

Starting with a specific project is a smart choice for Sean and Marielena. The service learning project is a good fit for the collaboration between the librarian and teachers across subject areas. The makerspace and library offer the space, resources, equipment, and technology to meet students' needs and provide inspiration. For "marketing" purposes (thinking back to Sean and Marielena's interest in promoting the makerspace at the grade-level meeting), this is also a highly visible project that makes a clear connection across the library, "making," and cross-curricular goals. This is an instance of another conceptual bridge (bridge 1): libraries provide links across content areas to support interdisciplinary learning. Library experiences in the makerspace offer creative means of forging links among content areas. Modeling the makerspace as an accessible and useful option for instruction may garner interest and new makerspace collaborations.

High school principal Dr. Jesse Turner has observed his school's makerspace to be highly motivating for his students, who discover and pursue passions like music or robotics in the school library makerspace at his Virginia high school. This level of engagement produces more than pieces of music and engineering feats: he believes that the passion for creative endeavor motivates his students to come to school. The students want to be a part of these spaces and this independent learning, he reports, a desire exemplified through anecdotes of students who might not be so thrilled to attend Algebra 2—a fear that might have kept them from coming to school at one point in time. Now these students come to school and take Algebra 2, but also enjoy the chance to visit the music studio during free periods, or before or after school.[6] This is a spoonful of sugar, maybe, but also a lesson in doing things that might not be our favorite activities as a pathway to pursuing a passion. This same student may be prepared for the content and experience of general education courses in college on his or her way to a music degree and the specialized classes in the major. For more on college and career readiness, see "College and Career Ready in the School Library."

Given that the preceding example is oriented to the high school level, you may be wondering about makerspace projects for elementary and middle school students. Table 2.1 presents a few possibilities.

LEARNING COMMONS

Another notable movement in student-centered learning is the learning commons. Like the makerspace, the learning commons concept facilitates student inquiry, authentic learning, and collaboration, but without the specific engineering and design focus of the makerspace. Some school libraries use the term "learning commons" to rename the library; some introduce features of the learning commons and continue to call the space "the library." The most noticeable characteristic of the learning

College and Career Ready in the School Library

In the aptly named article, "Graduating Students Who Are Not Only Learned But Also Learners," Jean Donham cites Newmann, Secada, and Wehlage in emphasizing the importance of learning activities that engage students in "using their minds well."[7] She explains that teachers must aim student work "toward production of discourse with value beyond success in school."[8]

Across subject areas and grade levels, school library programs provide consistent, cumulative practice of competencies that prepare students for college, vocational training, workforce education, and careers. Here are a few specific examples of the library program's alignment to the Common Core State Standards' picture of the college and career ready student, with CCSS skills italicized.[9]

These students *demonstrate independence and build strong content knowledge* via library inquiry tasks that require reading and applying informational texts to tasks designed for deep understanding. These interactions with texts from various sources require that students *comprehend as well as critique*. The CCSS tenet of *valuing evidence* is a central part of evaluating information, a regular component of information literacy instruction in the library.

Similarly, using *technology and digital media strategically and capably* is an everyday part of information seeking (through online catalogs, search engines, and reference databases) as well as interaction with information (collecting and organizing with digital tools and creating and sharing content). Students *respond to varying demands of audience, task, purpose, and discipline* by creating media products, written evidence, and other performance-based works to show the results of their inquiry processes for authentic purposes within subject areas and for audiences in the school setting and beyond.

Several library-based skills align well with the CCSS college and career readiness attribute of *understanding other perspectives and cultures*. One opportunity to develop this understanding is through reading and viewing materials in the library collection, selected to represent diverse voices and points of view. Further, self-assessment is a disposition emphasized in library instruction. This collection of skills and behaviors addresses the assessment of one's own work products, as might be expected, but it also includes assessment of information literacy processes. Consideration for the cultural and social context of information is a self-assessment strategy, as is the application of feedback from peers and teachers.[10]

Table 2.1 Makerspace projects across grade levels and subject areas

Grade level and subject areas	Project or lesson	Classroom, library, and makerspace activities
Kindergarten: Health and Physical Education	Make a video about rules and safe play in an outside game	Learn game rules; plan actions and dialogue for video script; practice and film video; upload and share
Grade 3: Social Studies, ELA	Identify and map places of personal significance	Discuss concept of place; write and draw about places of importance; find place locations on a map; construct a print or digital place map
Grade 6: Family Consumer Science, Art, ELA	Write and construct picture books for a babysitting unit	Create genre- and audience-specific writing; produce artwork; upload and digitize art; construct print books
Grade 8: Science, Math	Build a water filtration system to test and compare to natural filtering by oysters	Research oysters and mechanical water filtration; build water filtration; observe and test; document results

commons is arguably the layout, where collaborative spaces and furniture befit cooperation and different kinds of activities happening simultaneously. The learning commons reframes the library as a room with bookshelves and seating for "library lessons" and "book borrowing" into a flexible, busy, and exciting hub equipped for a range of learning activities.

Learning commons typically have big tables with movable chairs or benches (like the furniture on casters in the opening vignette), comfortable seating for reading or using devices, and whiteboards for sketching ideas, all usually in configurations that can be moved and changed easily to accommodate different activities and groupings of students. Also integral to the learning commons is access to technology equipment and networks. The resources extend out into the virtual space, such that students can access the tools for creativity, information, and productivity within or outside the physical space. The librarian's responsibility to build and maintain student access to materials reflecting diverse topics and formats is critical in the learning commons, because of the independence and personalized learning associated with this model of school library.

The learning commons is a dynamic physical space and rich online learning community, but it also might be described as an attitude. Flexibility, risk taking, and trust in students are required to make the concept work. Like the makerspace, teacher buy-in is essential for spreading this "attitude" throughout the school, especially at the middle school and high school levels, where school librarians' ability to work with students depends on teachers' willingness to schedule library time with their classes. Thus the learning commons attitude—or perhaps, the professional disposition—is required not only of the librarians who facilitate this work, but also of classroom teachers and school principals, who orchestrate and approve the practical matters that allow the learning commons to run.

With the burden of vast amounts of content to teach in a small span of time, teachers may be reluctant to try the learning commons or makerspace. But when school librarians—with the support of school leaders—can offer to share the work, teachers benefit from the shared responsibilities, school curricula become more cohesive, and students gain transferable college, career, and life skills. Learning commons, makerspaces, and other iterations of today's best school libraries make efficient use of school resources by locating them centrally in the school, granting access to all students and teachers, and through the librarian's familiarity with the curriculum across subjects and grade levels, facilitating collaborative instruction with sound academic rationale and rigor.

Professor David Loertscher is perhaps the school library field's leading proponent of the learning commons. His work consistently emphasizes the librarian's role as instructional partner and teacher in embedded, collaborative inquiry taught as part of the content-area curriculum.

Writing in *The Virtual Learning Commons*, Loertscher and colleagues explain, "[The learning commons] is designed to move students beyond mere research, practice, and group work to a greater level of engagement through exploration, experimentation, and collaboration."[11]

It's clear to see why many librarians embrace the concept of the learning commons: they adopt the "commons" from the academic or public library—the equity and access inherent in a "commons," the gathering and social functions—and leverage all this toward the mission of a school. The learning commons approach (meaning not just the space but the learning) exemplifies all three "bridges" that I suggested to illustrate how the library serves school goals: building content-area connections, technology and transliteracy skills, and collaborative, accountable communities of learners. The learning commons is an especially apt setting for growing transliteracy skills. The "learner who is transliterate builds knowledge, communicates, and interacts across a range of platforms, tools, and media," according to school library educator and researcher Gail Bush. That range of platforms, tools, and media is what the varied spaces and activities of the learning commons are designed to offer. Here, Bush points out where the "commons" fits into transliteracy, as students learn to "maintain an open, mindful, and critical approach to information and ideas while staying cyber-vigilant for oneself and ensuring the best possible outcome for oneself and the community of learners."[12]

Superintendent Mark Edwards describes the importance of learning to collaborate in *Every Child, Every Day*:

> Learning to collaborate as a team—using blogs, discussion boards, wikis and more—is engaging for young learners. It also prepares them for their future, and they know it. But people often make the mistake of assuming that kids know how to collaborate from day one. They do not. Developing team skills in collaborative working groups has to be part of the curriculum.[13]

The learning commons (and makerspaces, too) provide the community and collaboration orientation for the existing curriculum to thrive.

Learning commons make learning visible, according to librarian Chad Stephenson, describing the vision of the learning commons that he helped to implement at his school.[14] So what are these visible displays of learning in the commons? For the current discussion of student-centered learning, let's begin with these foundational elements: flexible access, student responsibility and personalized learning, and levels of implementation of the commons. In chapter 4, we'll take a closer look at some subject-specific examples of inquiry-based lessons for libraries, makerspaces, and learning commons.

FLEXIBLE ACCESS

Flexible access to the learning commons means access to space, resources, and people. Space includes the library room, including the furniture and options for configuring and using the room. Space can also mean virtual space, as in online collaboration rooms, shareable documents, and tools for chatting via text, audio, and video. Resources encompass the print library collection and online content, including databases, websites, applications, and e-books. People are the teachers, students, librarians, other educators in the building, and experts, community members, and instructors or collaborators who contribute remotely to student learning.

As I've described, the space in the learning commons is flexible in configuration. Flexibility also refers to schedule. A flexible library schedule allows teachers and librarians to schedule class time outside the restraints of a strict cycle. Flexible schedules are more common at the middle and high school levels. Elementary library schedules tend to be fixed, which can prevent optimum use of the learning commons, since teachers drop off students and don't participate in the library learning. School librarian Jennifer Reed works with a "fixed-flex" schedule in her elementary school library, with both scheduled classes and blocks of "flextime."[15] With the flextime and some creative scheduling efforts, like having teachers swap weeks of library class for extra-long classes (meaning teachers give up library class in some rotations so they can schedule longer classes), she gets the benefit of more continuous time with students for projects and chances to co-teach with classroom teachers. I'll talk more about different iterations of library schedules in chapter 7.

Flexible access also means access to the library materials wherever, whenever, at any time, in any format. In addition to the online catalog pointing to published print and nonprint items in the collection, the library's presence in the online space includes resources developed by teachers, the librarian, and other collaborators, such as the school counselor, principals, community partners, and students. Library portals personalize the online presence of the school library by guiding students to assignment instructions, online content, subject pathfinders, recommended apps and tools, style guides, public library resources, and samples of student work.

Teachers and librarians explicitly teach students (and whenever possible, parents and families) to go to these focused resources, which can be a tough sell with students who tend to use Google for every information need. Using tools for content curation places the information that librarians want kids to have in the formats that they tend to prefer: multimedia, browsable, quick, and connected to social networks. If teachers commit to constructing worthwhile but potentially complicated learning experiences in the makerspace and learning commons, then the right materials and the expert guidance to find and use them are critical.

CURATION OF RESOURCES AND TECHNOLOGIES TO SUPPORT INQUIRY

A collection management skill that I learned when I went to library school was making "vertical files"—a collection of articles, pamphlets, posters, brochures, and photographs maintained in file cabinets to support student and teacher information needs. The topics were often those visited year after year, including elections, health, endangered animals, authors, and weather. The files were easily accessed, suitable for adding local or regional items of interest, relatively cheap to supply and maintain, and efficient for everyone.

Before widely available Internet access, this kind of collection was a key supplement to books, periodicals, and, where available, computer-based reference databases, offering dynamic, responsive, localized content. Today's version of this student-focused resource collection retains the specificity and easy access of the old vertical file, only it now exists in the form of a curated digital collection. Researcher, educator, and former school librarian Joyce Valenza describes today's curation as "the selection and assembly of a focused group of resources into a Web-based presentation that meets an identified purpose or need and has meaning and context for a targeted audience."[16] Today's librarians use curation tools for building collections, sometimes in the form of content-specific instructional guides known as "pathfinders," for the school community as a critical part of their work.

For simplicity, we might think of today's curation for school libraries as having two constituent elements in states of nearly continuous update and motion. One element is the "stuff"— the array of multimedia content available for free or via paid license, online or on library shelves, or shared with classrooms and partner libraries. The other element of today's curation is the digital tools, usually free online applications accessed via computer or mobile device, which have replaced the file cabinet for organization of content, and this is where curation gets very exciting, powerful, and interesting.

At their most basic functionality, curation tools enable list making or direct embedding of selected content, such as articles, websites, videos, and images. Today's digital curation tools offer various options and organizational features for this collecting, but they are also made for and fueled by sharing; in fact, most tools are best leveraged through social features that help users build content, find sources, and evaluate information. Instead of the rather small circle of sharing that the vertical file offered, digital curation tools foster information sharing through networks of people and their information channels, like blogs, tweets, and their own lists and collections. Many tools provide options for leaving commentary (from the curator or other viewers) or ranking. Similar to how the vertical files were kept for specific classroom activities, digital curation collections provide utility for intended users and, when done well, encourage further investigation of the topic through connections made across resources. If students and teachers already know some of these tools from personal use, then librarians can use that familiarity and relevance as a chance to make a bridge from informal learning environments to the school setting.

Curation is the sifting, evaluating, and bridging of forms of information in creative, purposeful ways:

> Content exploration and learning demands a mix and match approach of networked conversation, collaboration and content curation, which means that a school librarian has to be intrinsically linked to effective and responsive information curation and dissemination in distributed environments within and beyond the school.[17]

Thus, today's curation is social. Organizing information to be shared within school (from librarian to students, from students to each other, from students to teachers) and outside of school (from the local and global community, experts, and learners to students, and from students to the local and global community) is the whole idea. Thankfully, digital curation tools are much more mobile than file cabinets! See the sidebar for examples of curation tools and collections.

STUDENT RESPONSIBILITY AND PERSONALIZED LEARNING

In this section, we'll look at examples of personalized learning experiences in the school library or learning commons, specifically, flipped

Curation Tools and Collections

Some of my favorite curation tools are Pinterest, Scoop.it, List.ly, paper.li, Delicious, Blendspace, bit.ly, and Learnist. The tools vary in social media integration (i.e., how lists can be shared or how users can comment or vote), layout (i.e., visual or text-based), and how the lists are populated. List.ly and Learnist work well when adding websites that users already know about. Paper.li and Scoop.it have features where users add keywords, Twitter feeds, or other RSS feeds to help identify content for the collection. Not to be forgotten is the use of others' curated collections, usually searchable on these sites or sometimes highlighted as recommended collections. Here are a few examples of content curation collections created by librarians and by students.

Examples of Librarian-Curated Collections

- Outcomes of Supreme Court decisions in local news
- Tools for digital storytelling
- Research style guides
- Book recommendations
- Resources for selecting plants for schoolyard habitat
- College and career guidance resources

Examples of Student-Curated Collections

- Healthy meals when eating out
- Free summer activities for teens
- Favorite author, illustrator, or genre-related websites
- Sources for science project ideas
- Resources for inquiry projects: presidential speeches, political conflicts, diaspora, biomes, astronomy, automobile mechanics

instruction and digital badging. There's an inherent expectation for student participation and accountability when setting up individualized learning resources and opportunities like those in the learning commons. Online learning through 1:1 initiatives, mobile device labs, and policies that allow students to use their own devices at school share this expectation. They also line up with the ways that students are accustomed to learning outside of school: young people have an affinity and seemingly natural inclination for technology-based activities and tools. Ninety-five percent of American teens are online. Three in four teens access the Internet through mobile devices, and ownership of smartphones and tablets by teens has grown substantially since 2011 (37 percent in 2013, up from 23 percent in 2011, according to the Pew Internet Research Project).[18]

Blue Valley High School's "satellite study hall" program offers a helpful example of independent learning opportunities in the library. An English teacher is available each period in the library to offer tutoring, similar to the services of a writing center. Like the writing center model, it's up to the students to take advantage of the expertise of the English teacher. This is part of library learning, too: identifying a need and seeking the help or information to address it. At the time of this writing, plans were under way at Blue Valley for math teachers to become part of the tutoring schedule of the satellite study hall.[19]

Flipped Instruction

Superintendent Mark Edwards writes that in his school district, "We believe that relevant, personalized, collaborative, and connected learning experiences enhance student engagement, which in turn drives student achievement."[20] A growing strategy that reflects these qualities of teaching and learning is flipped instruction. Flipped instruction methods vary in format and pedagogy, but they typically involve having students view a teacher-developed instructional segment, sometimes with tutorial or quiz sections, prior to coming to class. The "flip" is that this segment represents the "lecture" component that would normally happen in a face-to-face class. The learning activities that are typically "homework"—the practice problems, equations, analysis, or other interactions with the content—take place in school, with teachers present to guide and support students when they need intervention and instruction. Flipped instruction pioneers Jonathan Bergmann and Aaron Sams cite the following outcomes of flipping their classrooms: enhanced differentiation of instruction and keener knowledge of student needs, more student-to-student interactions, increased transparency of lessons and learning to the community, and changes in focus of parent communication, including more concentration on learning than behavior and family interest in school content.[21]

School library resources can enhance teachers' flipped learning initiatives with recommendations of vetted content for teachers to incorporate into their recorded instruction and for students to read and use. Librarians can also provide guidance and professional development training in the media production process. If flipping classes is an idea your teachers have been considering or are starting to try, you might introduce the librarian's technology and presentation expertise to subject-area teachers potentially less likely to turn to the library for instruction and collaboration. For instance, mathematics is a subject prime for flipping, but math teachers often don't use the school library. Having teachers record the instructional portion of a skill for students to view before class frees valuable time in class for one-on-one math help. The media production processes for recording and posting the flipped content are skills right in the librarian's professional development wheelhouse. In a teacher prep period or focused afterschool workshop—or in a flipped segment itself—librarians can teach the key steps in flipping content, and guide teachers to design and share instructional segments. Maximizing class time for hands-on practice, questions, individualized or small-group instruction, and immediate feedback is a huge advantage for math teachers, and teaching teachers how to attain that is an example of a different way for the library and librarian to add value to the school community.

Flipping works for content normally taught in the classroom, such as math skills or novels in ELA, but it is also effectively used directly in library lessons. For instance, a "flippable" segment of the ninth-grade service learning project is search strategies for local community and government organizations. The librarian might record sample searches with narrated screen capture video, modeling suggested search terms or Twitter hashtag searches, and demonstrating how to use the websites that students find. Having watched this instruction ahead of a class library visit, the students can then start their visit with a brief check-in and get right to work using those strategies.

At the middle school level, a flip could work in a seventh-grade introductory world language class, where students learn a set of new vocabulary words and phrases in teacher-made videos, then come to class to practice new phrases in dialogue with classmates. At the elementary school level, students and parents together could watch student-made book trailers to help guide student book choice during library circulation time.

Badging Individual Learning Experiences

Furthering the individualized learning experiences afforded by 1:1 initiatives and flipped instruction, digital badges offer another way for students to pursue areas of specialty that may require expert facilitation and review of work. As described by the Alliance for Excellent Education, "A badge is a digital credential that represents an individual's skills, interests, and achievements. Among other uses, badges can convey an individual student's core academic content knowledge, as well as other twenty-first-century competencies that cannot be measured by traditional assessments."[22]

A leader in the badge movement is Mozilla, whose open-source badge program allows organizations to create and issue badges with "data built in that links back to the issuer, the criteria it was issued under and evidence verifying the credential."[23] Users collect badges in digital "backpacks," which serve as dynamic collections of experiences and skills that may not be reflected by existing formalized systems of scoring or evidence. As the Alliance for Excellent Education report explains, the badge ecosystem comprises badge earners, badge issuers, and badge consumers.[24] This "highly individualized, peer-supported, and goal-oriented" strategy for credentialing learning codifies and enables students' informal learning experiences.[25]

How might badging be introduced into the ninth-grade service learning project, and for what purposes? The process of identifying one's badge-worthy skills is an exercise in self-assessment. Badging may also serve as another means of easing teachers' hesitation about projects requiring lots of new tools and skills. Divergent learning paths and tools are characteristic of inquiry in both learning commons and makerspaces, but this variety in student activities may be disconcerting for educators more accustomed to consistency in their pupils' work processes and products. Earning badges that encourage and recognize students' self-assessment and at the same time signify their willingness to help others is a concept highly aligned with the ideals of the learning commons: collaboration, accountability for one's self and others, and honoring different ways of knowing. And this works in similar ways for teachers, as described in the sidebar "Badging and Flipping with Teachers."

In participant-observation research that I conducted with intermediate and middle school students doing media production, certain students in each class emerged as experts in project steps like mixing music, inserting images, and saving files.[26] A similar approach could be applied with the ninth graders, wherein students self-identify or nominate peers with special expertise to earn badges. The badges could be displayed on a project wiki or website set up for requests for guidance. A system like this also adds another layer of authenticity to the students' learning.

Badging and Flipping with Teachers

Badging holds promise for teachers' professional learning endeavors as a means of tracking competencies gained in school-situated or externally offered professional development. For example, the University of Michigan School of Information's "Michigan Makers Team" facilitated the badging of a school library state conference in Ohio. Attendees filled out brief exit slips after participating in conference sessions, then submitted the slips as evidence of their learning in order to earn digital badges. Some attendees used the badges to remember what they learned, or to demonstrate participation at the event to administrators back at school.[27] This might be a useful model to try within your school at welcome-back in-service weeks, professional development boot camps, or training sessions held through the year. Teachers add badges to virtual backpacks or portfolios to track skills from continuing education or conferences they attend.

Teachers who are interested in online professional development will find that flipped instruction holds great potential for this avenue of learning. As with flipped instruction in K–12 learning, flipped professional development segments viewed before a face-to-face session allow synchronous time to be used for discussions, hands-on practice, or coaching. I flip much of the content for the online graduate courses that I teach. I record a content-focused briefing using the multimedia tool VoiceThread. Students view the briefing and read assigned articles before joining together for a synchronous weekly meeting. When we're together, students participate in interactive exercises, simulations, or other collaborative, live learning activities.

What might you be able to accomplish by flipping an in-service session, or even a faculty meeting? Perhaps you might deliver regular updates in a flipped segment, and use the time together to build collaborative partnerships, hold a dialogue, or teach a new technology tool.

In considering badge implementation at the elementary level, it is important to make a distinction between "traditional" incentive programs that track students' progress toward the same goals (e.g., number of pages read, math facts memorized, physical fitness milestones reached) versus progress toward independently determined goals. These might be classroom experts in technology tools or group work skills; sports and fitness strategists, teachers, or referees; or go-to students for classroom routines or schoolwide expertise, such as pet care, welcoming new students, or safety.

LEVELS OF IMPLEMENTATION OF THE LEARNING COMMONS

Even if you aren't currently in a position to make major changes to your library space, you can still implement key aspects of the learning commons philosophy with your teachers and librarian, and reap the student-centered learning benefits. A shift to a learning commons doesn't have to mean a renovation; the learning commons is perhaps as much about the attitude toward flexible access and formats, collaboration, and cross-curricular connections as it is about the physical space. As librarian Shannon Hyman describes in her school's library transformation, learning commons involve "restructuring existing notions about libraries as storage spaces and constructing a vision of the space as a scaffold to support both formal and informal learning experiences simultaneously." Further, Hyman emphasizes, her team's decisions about the design of the learning commons centered on people, flexibility, and durability.[28]

As you and your librarian consider how to introduce the learning commons or makerspace approach to your school, start by identifying existing teacher collaborators and the student learning objectives co-taught with the librarian. In dialogue with the teachers and librarians, reflect on these lessons and outcomes, and consider how the elements of a learning commons philosophy might enhance the learning. Would a longer block of time be useful, for instance? Perhaps a schedule swap would be an option. Are students asking for lots of help with a particular project component—citing sources, interviewing a family member, finding images, or reading a primary source document? Record a flipped segment for viewing and reviewing, and have one teacher work with small groups as others who are ready for other steps work independently. Did students have mixed reactions to working in large groups versus partners? Perhaps allow for student choice in group size, and ask the custodian to help slide tables to accommodate different combinations of learners. Allow students to work in either the classroom or the library, and develop a safety procedure for knowing which students are where. And of course—ask students what they want to see and how they want to work in the learning commons or makerspace.[29]

Honoring students' ideas, and especially their technology knowledge, is an important step in adopting a learning commons approach. Whether they are communicating through gaming, gleaning subject knowledge from members of a niche community, or creating content with media production tools, young people are comfortable with, if sometimes green at, many of the same skills that characterize today's work and social environments: heavy emphases on information technology, collaboration, problem solving, entrepreneurial thinking, and innovation. These students find guidance, tools, and acceptance from libraries and librarians. Every day in school libraries, students apply to academic activities the technology skills that they have honed through everyday tasks. They bring expertise across a myriad of technology competencies to their peers and teachers, and they learn from adults how to utilize and further their technology skills in ways that are smart, safe, and innovative. From their experiences in the library, they return to those games, online communities, and creative projects with refined skills and acknowledgment of their work.

School library educator and researcher Jami Biles Jones developed a Manifesto of Creative Inquiry, a list of belief statements for school librarians to follow in striving to foster students' creative potential through inquiry. This tenet rings especially true, not only for school librarians, but also for school leaders: "Students will take creative chances when it is safe to do so. Your job is to create a joyful school library environment that nurtures exploration, innovation, and questioning."[30]

Librarians and teachers can collaborate not only to design lessons, but also to engineer opportunities for students to participate creatively and independently. With the support of school leaders, teachers and librarians can create spaces and communities that place students at the center of their learning.

CHAPTER 3

Reading Across the Curriculum

Fostering Literacy and Transliteracy Skills

Stamina for Third-Grade Reading

Elementary school principal Angela's district-level curriculum supervisor has just announced that reading stamina will be the focus of the next professional development (PD) day for all grade levels, all teachers. With more research data and teachers' observations suggesting that students are having difficulty attending to and reading longer, more complex texts, the district administration has decided that an "all-hands" strategy is needed in reading instruction to help students "build energy and strength to do something for a long time."[1]

The schedule for the professional day has the teachers meeting first by grade levels or departments to identify current learning activities that support reading stamina. Then teachers will report out to share the learning activities already in place and lessons that might be strengthened to fit this goal. Finally, the teachers will meet in new combinations of grade-level bands and interdepartment groups to make specific plans to integrate reading stamina into an existing unit or new learning experience, possibly across disciplines. The district principals have been asked to assign their special area teachers to the groups where they think they will be a good fit. Angela is deciding where to assign Janine, the school librarian.

Angela is new to the school this year, and in her experience, the school librarian's role and expertise are primarily related to providing resources for reading. Librarians match reading levels and interests to requests from teachers and students, promote reading, and maintain a good library collection. Angela knows these are all important services, but without a clear, direct role in instruction for the librarian, Angela can't decide where Janine fits into the reading stamina day. She is starting to compose an e-mail to Janine with a proposal for her to spend the day checking in at the grade-level meetings to inquire about books needed, when she sees that Janine has already written to her.

Hi, Angela—

I'm looking forward to the upcoming professional development day on reading stamina. I wanted to mention to you that I've been working on a collaborative unit with the third-grade teachers on The Stories Julian Tells, *by Ann Cameron. This chapter book series has been popular with our middle readers for many years, and the teachers have started to build some whole-group activities around the stories. Last year I led some library storytelling to complement the classroom lessons, and this year the teachers and I were going to try some co-teaching, with read-alouds, sustained silent reading, and text-based discussions.*

The Stories Julian Tells *is an example of a complex text for second and third graders, and with our PD day coming up, I thought that our unit would fit right into the discussion! If possible, could you schedule me with the third-grade teachers so that we can align this unit with the reading stamina initiative? It would be a great chance for some collaborative planning. I appreciate your consideration, and please let me know if you'd like to hear more about our ideas.*

Many thanks,

Janine

•

Angela appreciates Janine's enthusiasm, but she isn't familiar with this practice of having the librarian co-teach reading, rather than act in support of reading. Is this something new, or just a skill unique to Janine? Are other teachers co-teaching with the librarian? Angela is intrigued, so she composes a response agreeing to Janine's suggestion, and makes a mental note to spend some of the PD day with third grade to see what this collaboration is all about.

LIBRARIES STRENGTHEN LITERACY EFFORTS

Reading is a primary emphasis in student learning outcomes and school performance results for school principals like Angela and for other school leaders like the curriculum supervisor in this vignette. Reading is a foundational skill for student achievement and a highly scrutinized and publicized measure of student success. No matter the impetus for a particular school or system's literacy focus, reading is an ongoing high priority across school leaders, and not just for the leaders of English or reading departments.

This section begins with a wide-lens look at how the school library program and schoolwide literacy initiatives intersect. I then suggest how to align the people and resources in your school for maximum literacy learning outcomes, with a special focus on three dimensions of literacy instruction: reading stamina, engaging with content-based informational texts, and transliteracy in reading instruction. First, let's examine the relationship between school library programs and literacy programs.

The Common Core State Standards "insist" (as the document describes) that literacy instruction be a shared responsibility across teachers. This approach is reflected in the organization of the standards, in which one of the two sections of grades 6–12 English language arts (ELA) standards is designed for instructing literacy skills as they pertain to science, social studies, and technical subjects.[2]

A shared responsibility for literacy instruction is also reflected in the *Remodeling Literacy Learning* report, a nationally representative survey of educators of varied roles, grade levels, and subject areas conducted by the National Center for Literacy Education. The report shows that 76.7 percent of the 2,404 K–12 educators surveyed agreed or strongly agreed that "developing students' literacy is one of the most important parts of [their] job[s]." This report also identifies librarians and literacy coaches as professionals specifically designated as having "a critical role in building schools' collective capacity to improve literacy learning."[3]

In this context, I think of capacity building as the opportunity and impetus to increase potential for student learning and for teacher excellence. School librarians build capacity in students and teachers by fulfilling an active and varied role in teaching literacy, beyond the expected services of providing books and supporting research. Like Janine in the opening vignette, many school librarians are already working to teach and co-teach schoolwide literacy initiatives. Angela's decision to grant Janine's request to spend the PD day with the third grade teachers is a promising outcome. If we play out this scenario more fully, we might see Angela participate in the third-grade meeting herself to learn about the ongoing planning and provide support. Her participation might raise the eyebrows of the teachers, but it could also introduce new thinking about the logistics of the project. What forms of help could the teachers request from Angela to make the ideas work? Maybe the scheduling of the project is a concern. How can Angela help them fit the co-teaching elements into the school schedule? Materials are another potential topic. Are there sufficient numbers of *The Stories Julian Tells* for all students? Extending the project beyond the classroom teachers and librarian might be of interest to Angela. Are there other teachers, maybe art or physical education, who also might connect this unit to their curricula?

As these topics suggest, inviting a school leader into this planning process stands to produce additional benefits besides answering Angela's literacy day scheduling dilemma and granting Janine's request to spend time with third grade. Janine has professional dispositions and skills that lend to literacy and reading, and the observations and insights of the school principal during this meeting can channel those skills toward needed areas in the school. The library has a schoolwide reach that encompasses and serves all teachers, students in all grade levels, and all curricula. Perhaps this is a scope not fully realized at the current time, but it is accessible with some purposeful and creative planning. As principal, Angela has a deep knowledge of the curriculum, a necessarily big-picture mind-set, and influence in the school that will allow her to optimize opportunities for student learning (like this third-grade unit) in collaboration with the school library and librarian. The existing professional expertise, resources, and mission of the school library can be applied to attain the critical, priority school goal of shared, purposeful, and effective literacy instruction.

An effective school library program shows correlational relationships to achievement in student reading and writing.[4] It stands to reason that school leaders would desire and value the contributions that a strong school library can make to students' reading and writing skills. As the Pennsylvania School Library Project found, "Students performed better on reading and writing tests in schools where the principal placed high value on the librarian collaborating with teachers in planning and teaching and providing in-service education to teachers, met regularly with the librarian, and appointed the librarian to serve on key school committees."[5] With this student achievement potential in mind, let's examine more closely how the library's existing priorities and practices complement and strengthen reading instruction at the school level.

HOW CONNECTED ARE YOUR LIBRARY AND LITERACY PROGRAMS?

It's a quick and mostly reasonable hypothesis that libraries and reading go hand in hand. It is true that reading is a fundamental and readily identifiable aspect of most school library programs, but not necessarily for the same reasons or with the same depth of impact from school to school. From their beginnings, school libraries and media centers have served students and teachers with books, resources, and programming to promote and foster reading. Alongside and intertwined with the technology tools and skills that vie for librarians' and students' attentions, today's school library programs are oriented toward reading today and reading for life.

The first of the school library profession's nine Common Beliefs, introduced in chapter 1, states that "reading is a foundational skill for learning, personal growth, and enjoyment." With lifelong learning as a shared goal of K–12 education and school libraries, intentional alignment of reading initiatives and the library program can serve that objective. Let's consider what that may look like by matching up the library's reading services and instruction with efforts at the school level. I have proposed a continuum (see table 3.1) to illustrate approaches to the integration of reading instruction and the library program. Note that these are examples used for discussion, and that school libraries may have characteristics representing different points on the continuum, rather than exclusive matches.

At the far left end of this continuum, the school library is a space for teaching and reading, and primarily serves as a resource center with curriculum-aligned and other materials. At this point in the continuum, the association between library and reading is mostly that the library is "where the books are located." Through either your current school or other school settings, you're probably familiar with libraries that function primarily for students to borrow books to read, most likely through a scheduled class during teacher prep time or during students' free periods or study time. This is the frame of reference of Angela, the principal in the opening vignette. The librarian promotes reading through seasonal and thematic displays, events, contests, and clubs. Through the weekly classes, students learn about and borrow

Table 3.1 Continuum of library and schoolwide literacy program integration

Minimal integration of library and literacy →				**Maximum integration of library and literacy**
Library functions as a resource center Book borrowing and literacy programs are mostly separate	Teachers and librarians coordinate content to some extent Librarian maps collection to curriculum	Librarian and ELA teachers share resources, co-plan instruction	Librarian supports ELA curriculum development	Literacy is fully integrated into the library program Librarians and teachers co-plan and often co-teach literacy learning Librarian leads professional development on literacy and inquiry

books that reflect highlighted genres, topics, authors and illustrators, and other focal points. The library may support a school policy of carrying a book at all times, in case students or teachers find extra minutes to read, or for reading during "Drop Everything and Read" (DEAR) sessions. Professional collections serve as a library of teacher resources.

At this end of the continuum, borrowing books and other materials for reading is mostly viewed as a separate, perhaps parallel, channel of activity from reading instruction. Admittedly, when I was a first-grade teacher, I had limited level involvement with my students' book borrowing from the school library. Looking back, my school librarian would probably have valued my input and support of students' independent reading choices. After all, I enjoyed first-grade teaching partly because of the children's literature for that age group. However, in some circumstances, a model of intentional, shared literacy instruction isn't in place. This useful, but not necessarily fully maximized library scenario offers support, resource, and enrichment to the literacy program. The use of the word "support" here is most intentional; to "support" an initiative is good, but support doesn't imply a vital role. In fact, I caution my school library candidates about their use of that word. Lending support sounds nice, but it also sounds expendable. Library programs should be indispensable in literacy instruction.

Moving toward the right-hand side of the library and literacy integration continuum, we find additional, purposeful practices that expand the basic elements of a library program out into the school. In varying iterations, schools may incorporate practices such as the following in order to build a more cohesive and effective approach to literacy. You'll notice that these practices involve training, communication, and a presence outside the library.

- Training in the reading program or district-adopted reading strategies for school librarians
- Schedule that supports librarian and classroom teacher co-teaching and co-planning
- Literacy or ELA team that incorporates school librarians, literacy coaches, and reading specialists in addition to classroom teachers
- School librarians represented on curriculum planning committees
- Coordination between school leaders (principals, curriculum directors) and librarians on opportunities and expectations
- School librarians included in CCSS or other standards implementation, assessment preparation, and training

At the most developed end of the continuum, the school library, librarian(s), and library staff function as a dynamic, supported, and supportive hub of teaching and learning, information creation, and resources for students and teachers. This is the scenario that Janine would love to work toward. These valued-added components are the building blocks to a reading and literacy program that takes full advantage of the library, and in the last section of this chapter, we'll examine some instructional scenarios enabled by this foundation. But first, let's put in place the people and tools your school already has to work toward a level of robust, integrated, and responsive literacy instruction.

ALIGNING PEOPLE FOR MAXIMUM LITERACY INSTRUCTION

Ideally, school leaders work directly with the school librarian and other staff to position the school library program centrally in the school's literacy instruction in relation to reading. Student learning can benefit from strengthening and aligning the literacy instruction efforts of the teachers of reading, including the school librarian, reading specialists, and literacy coaches, as well as ELA instructors and classroom teachers across subject areas. First are the educators who are the "named" reading teachers in your building. These may be the ELA teachers, reading specialists, literacy coaches for student or teachers, and special education teachers. These are the teachers whose curriculum is deeply focused on literacy learning, and whose expertise may include English and literature studies in addition to the pedagogy for teaching reading, writing, listening, and speaking. These will be key persons to pull in to meet with the librarian given their areas, but sometimes these are the teachers who, paradoxically, don't use the library much or see much value other than the collection. It is important to recognize that these teachers are probably under great pressure to see their students perform. That the librarian strengthens the classroom teachers' ability to attain the rigors of the standards should be the focal point of any conversations with these teachers.

Next, we might think of those people who are also "teachers of reading," though perhaps not by official title or department. The Common Core State Standards place a strong emphasis on the reading of complex texts, particularly informational texts, in increasing proportions to literary texts as the standards progress through the grade levels. Reading informational texts, developing deep understanding, and using evidence to demonstrate learning are all essential tasks, not only within English language arts classes but also history/social studies, science, and technical subjects. However, time for thoughtful reading and comprehension of complex texts is a significant challenge to build into the school schedule, and these collaborative efforts can address that time crunch.

Finally, who are the teachers who work with students in unique settings and durations, such as more than one grade level in a room (e.g., an Advanced Placement class), more than one year of instruction with the same kids (e.g., a world language teacher), or more than one teacher teaching together (perhaps special education)? It's very possible that these people—unified arts or specialist teachers, school counselors, health and physical education teachers, special education teachers, and the school librarians—can also play key roles in integrated library and literacy instruction in your school.

With this constellation of people and priorities in view, let's talk through two significant dimensions of shaping this literacy team: the logistical and the interpersonal. The logistical often boils down to schedule, and a frequent limiter of collaboration is a lack of common time. Sometimes personal hesitations or perceptions make for a less visible role on the literacy team, or even on the faculty at large. When elementary librarians work at several buildings in a district, for instance, the rotating schedule creates a challenge in establishing a sense of belonging, not to mention allowing for time to get to know and meet with colleagues and school leaders. For two years of my middle school library position, I taught one period of first-grade library a week at another building in the district. Even by midyear, the school secretary sometimes didn't recognize me when I arrived to sign in, and I saw the principal and teachers only occasionally. It was challenging to find time to update and plan. I did my best to keep up with what colleagues were doing in the classroom, rather than understanding the broad context for contributing to current areas of focus.

Does your school library schedule serve as contractual teacher prep time? This was the case for my school back when I was a first-grade teacher; I usually spent the forty or so minutes of preparation time during the students' library class calling parents, setting up the next activity, or reviewing student work or behavior charts. As I walked my class back to the room from the library, I shared students' enthusiasm over books they checked out and took a glance. My interactions with the librarian were similarly quick, even rushed, as our class left and the next group came in. Aside from these casual exchanges and trying to help students remember which day was library day, as a classroom teacher, I didn't really have much to do with my students' book borrowing—even though reading instruction is a fundamental objective of first grade.

Consider my experience as a first-grade teacher—someone very interested in reading but without a structured forum for library collaboration—and imagine how many other professionals in the building were working with the same children and similar goals, all in their own spheres. If you see parallels with your school, consider what might happen if these efforts were more coordinated and aligned. What opportunities are out there just simmering? What scaffolding might school leaders provide to build more purposeful literacy instruction and collaboration? At a faculty meeting or grade-level meeting, why not conduct a practical exercise that opens up curriculum mapping across subject areas, including specials? Even by starting with one set of learning objectives, coordination and sharing among teachers stands to narrow the gap that tends to separate what could be more synchronized, rich efforts to teach literacy. As described in the discussion of bridges in chapter 1, library experiences can foster critical links across those domains.

Investing classroom teachers and special teachers in each other's work can serve as motivation, and dedicating meeting time to that task can turn motivation into actionable steps toward student learning. It's important to include librarians and other specialists in curriculum planning activities like the faculty meeting exercise suggested above. Due to scheduling difficulties or just the tendency to overlook these teachers, they might be less involved in committee roles, curriculum development and implementation, or technology integration initiatives, so opportunities to plan for more integrated instruction can be missed. In the action brief *Implementing the Common Core State Standards: The Role of the School Librarian*, David V. Loertscher and Kathryn Roots Lewis go so far as to suggest that specialists should be included in the school's leadership team:

> If the leadership team of the school includes all specialists who have a responsibility across the school, then as a team they can influence what is going on in every classroom, department, and curricular area. By integrating their own agendas with those of the classroom teachers, the specialists can have a larger impact than they otherwise could by carrying out a "curriculum" of their own.[6]

School leaders are positioned to help librarians and specialists turn typical organizational dividing lines into bridges that connect literacy learning opportunities. What might some of these opportunities look like?

STRATEGIES FOR ALIGNING LIBRARY PROGRAMS AND LITERACY INSTRUCTION

A few disclaimers are useful in setting up our next topic: instructional strategies that leverage the librarian and library program in an active, visible literacy instruction role work to the benefit of students across the school. The suggestions made assume reasonable expectations regarding the expertise of the school librarian and for content-area teachers outside of ELA, with the acknowledgment that ongoing, even challenging, professional development is an expectation of a teaching career. I don't wish to suggest that the librarian or any teaching faculty should serve as an aide or paraprofessional alongside the classroom teacher, or that administrators should assign teaching responsibilities that fall outside teachers' areas of certification. Rather, I want to help school leaders channel and maximize skills of the school faculty within the realm of realistic professional growth and organizational progress. No one is expecting the librarian to be a reading specialist (unless s/he really is one), but the librarian isn't just a helper, either.

Taking this perspective into account, let's also recognize that there are numerous reading programs and instructional approaches with great potential to be strengthened by the library program and the librarian's teaching. We'll concentrate here on three select concerns of reading and language arts instruction appropriate for library-situated instruction or as part of collaborative teaching and planning opportunities for teachers and librarians. For further examples and lesson plans for your reference and for your school librarians' professional reading, I recommend Judi Moreillon's books on co-teaching reading comprehension strategies in elementary and secondary school, as well as "The School Librarian's Role in Reading Toolkit," an American Association of School Librarians resource available free online at the AASL website.[7] Some of the strategies below are adapted and cited from these texts and the toolkit.

Introduction to the Examples

To set the stage for these examples, it is helpful to point out the three main instructional and assessment shifts introduced by the Common Core State Standards:

1. Complexity of texts and academic vocabulary
2. Reading, writing, and speaking grounded in evidence from texts

3. Building disciplinary knowledge from content-rich texts, particularly nonfiction[8]

Literature describing school librarians' roles in implementing the standards elaborates on these three areas by spreading out the skills across six categories, which creates a helpful reference for picturing the range of needs that stand to be addressed within the school's reading agenda. These categories are

1. Balancing informational and literary texts
2. Knowledge in the disciplines
3. Staircase of complexity
4. Text-based answers
5. Writing from sources
6. Academic vocabulary[9]

In the three examples that follow, I examine the library's potential role in teaching and supporting (1) reading stamina and self-monitoring/self-assessment skills, (2) close reading and text-based evidence, and (3) content-based informational texts, which all relate to strategies and skills that reflect instructional shifts within the ELA Common Core State Standards.

Example 1: Cultivating Reading Stamina

Reading stamina is an area that supports the staircase of complexity and academic vocabulary and builds habits of mind that strengthen reading skills. Working for reading stamina is not unlike striving for stamina in running or swimming; it is a process of building the energy, endurance, and self-discipline to sustain longer and longer durations of successful activity. For reading, "successful activity" is meaningful, real engagement with a text, which isn't necessarily a given during independent reading time in a classroom or the library. Such was a finding in a classroom study of sustained silent reading (SSR), in which Kelley and Clausen-Grace observed that some students were "fake readers," those struggling or disengaged readers who "read the words in a text without attaching meaning, or literally pretended to read."[10] It stands to reason that it would be hard to muster energy and motivation when a child isn't making meaning or "getting something" out of a text. Even the runner on a treadmill who's not really going anywhere gains value from the running: maybe progress toward being able to run a certain distance without stopping or meeting a goal of exercising so many days per week. The reader staring at a page doesn't gain much at all.

Librarians sometimes see this disengagement in students who aim to borrow and read "trophy" books before they're ready for them. Trophy books are the ones getting a lot of buzz at school, maybe commercially hot titles, recent books-to-film, or other books that earn recognition from parents or peers. The books aren't problematic in themselves, and it can be a great thing that students are talking about reading and sharing favorite stories. But keeping up with a book trend can pose legitimate barriers of reading readiness. For my first graders (and sometimes their parents) when I was a classroom teacher, the trophy books were the Harry Potter series. The first few titles might have had vocabulary within the students' reading levels, but most of my six- and seven-year-olds didn't have the accompanying comprehension skills to read and engage deeply in an independent reading experience with Harry Potter.

A situation like this is a chance for librarians and teachers to help students gain value from their reading experiences when kids may not be getting anywhere on their own. For the Harry Potter books, teachers and librarians could co-write a reading newsletter to parents, including ideas like read-alouds at home, with suggested prompts to talk about the story. With the librarian's knowledge of children's literature, the use of readers' advisory databases, and the teacher's knowledge of students' reading levels, they might also promote and read together (and suggest to parents in the newsletter) grade-level appropriate read-alikes and different stories about similar topics. This lets the students build positive reading experiences while they work their way up to more challenging stories.

Allington and Gabriel identify six "elements of [reading] instruction that every child should experience every day," which they assert "can be implemented in any district and any school, with any curriculum or set of materials, and without additional funds."[11] This accessible, schoolwide philosophy coordinates perfectly with the current discussion of supporting literacy by most effectively utilizing people and programs already in place. Among the activities of this research-based daily regimen are having every child read something he or she chooses every day, read this text accurately, and understand it. Allotting time for students to talk with peers about reading and writing is another suggested practice, beneficial because switching across tasks of reading, writing, speaking, and listening strengthens these skills. Not only will these practices support the library program's goal of nurturing lifelong reading skills, but following these recommendations aligns with the staircase of complexity in the standards, through which "students advancing through the grades are able to gain more from whatever they read."[12]

The aim of reading stamina is multilayered: teachers and librarians want to help students "endure" for longer periods of time, but not just for the sake of learning to sit still. The dimension of the goal is for students to gain something in the process, which is partly about the content knowledge or story, but also about developing awareness of what they are doing as they read, and constructing an identity of themselves as readers. Among the strategies that Kelley and Clausen-Grace taught to their students (including the "fake readers" mentioned earlier, along with more advanced readers) were skills in metacognition. In addition to teaching specific strategies, such as predicting or asking questions, they guided students to notice their thinking during reading and later talk to peers about how they applied the strategies.[13] This is a skill to discuss and plan for with teachers and specialists (perhaps another faculty meeting or online PD focus), so that students receive consistent reminders of reading strategies in the classroom, in the library, when reading in art or music, and during reading practice at home.

Taking note of progress in reading might also involve a literal tracking of progress, like having students list what they read on bookmarks or electronically for personal lists or class collections for sharing and recommending.[14] There is great authority in books recommended by peers, and a system that promotes peer sharing would be a fruitful project for the classroom teacher and librarian. Displays, blogs, student-made video book trailers, and shelf markers that show recommendations might be ways to promote reading between the classroom and library spaces, and build students' identities as people who read and talk about reading. I often tried to model and verbalize "what good readers do" with my first graders and middle schoolers. Good readers share and talk about reading, and that requires metacognitive skills.

In addition to the metacognition that supports reading skill development, librarians model and encourage students to have confidence to read outside their preferences and for different purposes. Our next area of focus is close reading, one purpose of which is also related to stamina and persistence, especially with those texts that aren't so "easily consumed."[15]

Example 2: Close Reading and Text-Based Evidence

Even by name, close reading doesn't sound like something that teachers and students have time to do in the blur that often characterizes a day of school. Thus, a librarian who shares or co-teaches close reading is supporting a need on multiple levels. Close reading is reading, rereading, and interacting with text to notice ideas, make connections, and ask and answer questions. This is a process that works well with instructional stages of direct instruction, modeling, guided practice, and independent practice, and it can be done with small groups or whole classes, in the library or classroom, with informational or literary texts. Harris describes the three rounds of close reading as a first round for comprehension, a second for rereading and answering higher-order questions (looking this time for specific evidence to support conclusions), and finally a third read, either independently or in a read-aloud, to facilitate more complex thinking about the literary elements and build associations with other texts, perspectives, or the author's purpose.[16]

In observations of ten secondary teachers (representing English, social studies, and science), Fisher and Frey identified five key features of close reading that differ from traditional reading instruction at the elementary level: short passages, complex texts, limiting frontloading (the preparation for what students are about to read), repeated readings with a purpose or question for each round, and text-dependent questions.[17] We'll study the secondary-level skills of annotation and note taking in the next section; here, let's narrow in on text-based evidence.

Using text-based evidence to answer a question or to support an argument is one of the key instructional shifts in the CCSS, and an area cited by numerous publications as one ripe for collaboration, coteaching, and leadership from the school librarian.[18] An approach for structuring the text-based questions as described by Fisher and Frey and also suggested by Walker and Shaw in *Teaching Reading Strategies in the School Library* is Raphael's Question-Answer Relationship. This approach guides students to figure out where or whether answers can be found directly in the text or if a different kind of analysis is needed in order to shape a response.[19] This approach can be interpreted with appropriate language for different grade levels. With the third-grade unit in the opening vignette, a way to encourage use of these strategies would be the posters and simple text recommended by Walker and Shaw to guide students through such scenarios as "Author and You," where "you cannot find the answer in the story. You need to think about what the author tells you, what you already know, and how it connects."[20] Using these posters in the classroom and library for the *Julian* lesson and then referring to them again for the next story is a simple and effective way to build a consistent approach to reading strategies across the library and classroom.

At the secondary level, close reading might be a useful strategy to practice when students are using library databases to find articles for research. A goal for the first reading could be for students to explain why they think the article will help answer their research question. Students base their responses on the first reading, focusing on text features, such as captions, title, subject headings, bold type, subheadings in the article, key words, abstract, and so on. The librarian could prepare a template for students to complete after their first reading, with topics and responses such as these:

QUESTION: What research question does your article help you answer?

STUDENT RESPONSE: This article has a map of where Islam is practiced in the world today, so I think that's going to help me answer where followers of this religion are concentrated geographically, and why I think this is so.

QUESTION: What key words made you select this article?

STUDENT RESPONSE: These words in the title and abstract tell me this is a good article for me: "fastest-growing religion" and "most populated countries."

In the second reading, maybe the next day, students follow up on these predictions with evidence from the article, in the form of note taking or note making. If the lesson is during a library class, the first part of the class would be spent reading independently, and perhaps the teacher and librarian check the students' worksheets from the first day. Then the students return to the worksheets after reading and reflect on their predictions. For instance, they could explain whether the title was true to the content, and what sections of the article helped answer their questions. Following instruction, perhaps in the form of a mini-lesson from the teacher or librarian, they start taking notes. The goal is to build an intentional process of reading and using information. Often, students find an article really quickly and then try to make it fit the research question, whereas close reading supports a more reflective and productive approach to student reading and research.

Close reading also serves to prepare students for the Common Core State Standards–related assessments, for which they must "read closely and critically to comprehend a range of increasingly complex literary and informational texts" in the Smarter Balanced Assessment Consortium and "read and comprehend a range of sufficiently complex texts independently" as part of the PARCC Assessment.[21]

Other ways in which your school librarian and library can support close reading are by providing a rich choice of texts in the library collection—"texts worth reading," as Wixson describes them.[22] This is a rich area of knowledge and resources from your school librarian, a long-standing expertise perhaps to be channeled for new purposes in the rigorous reading demands of today's academic standards. A topic relevant to "texts worth reading" is the classroom library collection; see the sidebar for what may be a new perspective on this topic.

In wrapping up our look at close reading, it should be noted that writing associated with close reading is another key area for library and teacher collaboration, including guiding students to read and use information from multiple sources. This is examined further in chapter 4, "Inquiry and Critical Thinking."

Example 3: Engaging with Content-Based Informational Texts

The CCSS K–5 ELA standards suggest that in the elementary setting, generally, one teacher in a self-contained classroom is providing the instruction for reading/writing/listening/speaking, math, science, and social studies. In the third-grade classroom of Janine's colleagues in the opening vignette, attending to comprehension strategies in reading a science text or having students write a journal entry from the point of

Classroom Library Collections

Classroom libraries can be a point of concern for school librarians, not because they don't want students to read, but because these smaller libraries are sometimes offered as substitutes for a school library, or they receive funding that might otherwise have purchased library resources to be used by the entire school. I am not saying to remove classroom libraries. Sometimes class sets of texts or materials used daily work well in the classroom or when shared by departments. Where I offer caution, though, is the development of expanded libraries for classrooms at the expense of print or electronic resources for the school library. School libraries, with the full complement of collaborative opportunities for instruction, a big picture of the curriculum horizontally and vertically, and efficient access provided to all students, offer a more integrated and economical alternative to individual classroom libraries.[23] School libraries also prepare students to anticipate and use the services and materials of other libraries, including the public library and academic libraries.

view of a historical figure are integrated reading activities across instruction in other content areas. In most cases, the same teacher teaches and knows well the pacing and progression of the students' literacy learning.

The grades 6–12 standards are organized into two separate sections for literacy learning—one, for literacy as it is taught in the reading, language arts, or English class, and a second section for literacy in other content areas. Thus the standards "reflec[t] the unique, time-honored place of ELA teachers in developing students' literacy skills while at the same time recognizing that teachers in other areas must have a role in this development as well."[24] The standards (and really, today's educational environment beyond the CCSS) demand a purposeful integration of literacy into student learning. Thus, secondary education teachers must teach their specialized subjects, in addition to literacy. There is much attention today to literacy in subject areas other than reading and ELA.

The school library program can effectively bridge literacy instruction, pulling together library skills related to research with the content-based reading emphasized in the CCSS, supporting the shift from literary to informational texts through the grade levels. Reading an informational text, whether as part of a group classroom lesson or as a phase of a more independent inquiry process, can be messy, in that a lockstep progression doesn't necessarily dictate what students should do to find information. Reading informational text is often iterative, requiring multiple reads of texts to clarify, break down, or make connections. The close reading process is not necessarily intuitive for readers, as questions evolve in light of new information, sources reveal surprises or insufficient detail, and unknown facts challenge what students thought they knew. Whether it's second graders discerning facts from opinion or high schoolers synthesizing numerous texts and multimedia sources to craft an argument, there are information-seeking skills, reading strategies, and content background knowledge involved in reading informational texts. This engagement with text to find information is within the expertise of the school librarian, and school leaders can help connect teachers to meet this need.

For example, you might find out which teachers are currently taking their classes to the library to "get research stuff" or request carts of books for classroom research use, and invite them to call upon the librarian's expertise more prominently. A common frustration of librarians is when teachers stop their library use after the start of an information-seeking process, maybe just requesting that the librarian show students the databases or books on a certain subject, without time to work on using the materials. If more time is dedicated to this part of reading for information, like the close reading and note-taking process described earlier, librarians can contribute to literacy goals in a focused way by teaching students to use informational texts of varied formats effectively to make meaning and build content knowledge.

Note taking is a good place to start these deeper collaborative efforts for teaching the reading of content-based texts because using specific evidence from close reading of texts to support ideas is already a characteristic of library research. Judi Moreillon describes the process of "note making" rather than note taking to emphasize a more active skill of interpreting content and adding insights and questions.[25] In library classes, in instructional segments in classrooms, or even through flipped learning segments made available for teachers' use as part of reading practice, teaching consistent note-taking and note-making skills across classes and curricula makes a strong impression on students and helps them to make some order out of their research and inquiry processes.

BRINGING IT ALL TOGETHER: TRANSLITERACY IN READING INSTRUCTION

There is another dimension of literacy relevant to this discussion, and your school librarians are probably already teaching it. As discussed in chapters 1 and 2, transliteracy brings together what we might call traditional reading skills with the kind of reading and writing enabled by and required for participation in today's technology and information environments. "Transliteracy" is the term that merges a seeming myriad of "other" literacies: digital, media, information, technology, even civic literacy.

As Thomas et al. describe in *First Monday* (the "peer-reviewed journal of the Internet"), transliteracy is the skill set that brings together "the ability to read, write and interact across a range of platforms, tools and media from signing and orality through handwriting, print, TV, radio, and film, to digital social networks." Further, "as a behavior, it is not new—indeed it reaches back to the very beginning of culture—but it has only been identified as a working concept since the Internet allowed humans to communicate in ways which seem to be entirely novel."[26]

Bush situates these media and technology skills in the context of teaching and learning, asserting that the alignment between the CCSS and transliteracy skills invites interdisciplinary partnerships for school librarians.[27] Although transliteracy as a term is not employed in the Common Core State Standards, the skills are reflected in the learning outcomes expected of students. See table 3.2 for an example of the alignment across sixth-grade reading standards and school library standards, including transliteracy skills.

There have long been aspects of transliteracy in the curriculum even without the layer of technology skills that current iterations of this skill set tend to infer. When students of history study and interpret photographs, speeches, articles, textbook chapters, journals, and primary source documents, they are practicing transliteracy skills by applying context-specific strategies to texts and media. As the information specialist, the librarian can teach this skill set by introducing teachers and students to resources that may not be as familiar as those on the free web. For example, librarians demonstrate the use of reference databases that students and teachers may not think to try first in a search. Then, through tasks co-planned with teachers, students learn to use information creatively so as not only to read and consume, but also to produce and create. We will see more examples of creative processes and products in the upcoming chapters.

When teachers and librarians guide students in engaging with texts across formats and other ways of "reading," they are building students' transliteracy skills. As we saw in preceding discussions and in the example with Angela and Janine that begins this chapter, when subject-area teachers collaborate with school librarians to plan and teach literacy, classroom teachers lead in their respective content instruction, and librarians take the lead in the "library and information" part. This part of the teaching and learning involves reading strategies, but it also

Table 3.2 Sample alignment of reading standards and school library standards

Common Core State Standards Reading: Informational Text	*Standards for the 21st-Century Learner,* American Association of School Librarians
CC.6.R.I.7 Integration of Knowledge and Ideas: Integrate information presented in different media or formats (e.g., visually, quantitatively) as well as in words to develop a coherent understanding of a topic or issue.[a]	1.1.6 Read, view, and listen for information presented in any format (e.g., textual, visual, media, digital) in order to make inferences and gather meaning.
	1.1.7 Make sense of information gathered from diverse sources by identifying misconceptions, main and supporting ideas, conflicting information, and point of view or bias.
	2.1.1 Continue an inquiry-based research process by applying critical thinking skills (analysis, synthesis, evaluation, organization) to information and knowledge in order to construct new understandings, draw conclusions, and create new knowledge.
	2.1.3 Use strategies to draw conclusions from information and apply knowledge to curricular areas, real world situations, and further investigations.[b]

a. National Governors Association Center for Best Practices, Council of Chief State School Officers, "Common Core State Standards, English Language Arts Standards" (Washington, DC: National Governors Association Center for Best Practices, Council of Chief State School Officers, 2010).

b. AASL, "Crosswalk of the Common Core Standards and the Standards for the 21st-Century Learner" (Chicago: ALA, 2011).

includes skills in changing modes of engagement: reading, viewing, listening, and writing. Librarians teach students how and when to access various formats of information, and they work with students to make meaning through curating, organizing, and creating new ways of building and sharing content.

When I was a school librarian, I really enjoyed finding new ideas for lesson plans, book discussions, projects, and web resources, and rolling out the new technologies and tools that I learned outside of school at conferences and library workshops. But without teacher partners, I never would have had any students with whom to use these ideas. Being centrally situated in a school community doesn't lead to automatic results. School librarians have much to offer in the way of literacy instruction, but they rely on their teaching colleagues and school leaders to help them put their resources and expertise to work for the most students. Now that we have considered how school leaders can situate the school library program for a more impactful role in literacy instruction, let's build on these collaborative strategies and integrated approaches to literacy by delving into student inquiry and critical thinking.

CHAPTER 4

Inquiry and Critical Thinking

Transforming the Culture of Learning

A Fair Question About Diversity

The monthly school faculty meeting is wrapping up. When Tim, the school principal, asks for any last announcements or questions, the second-grade team leader, Jane, introduces a concern with the upcoming annual Family Heritage Fair, which culminates their class unit on countries and cultures around the world. Each student constructs an exhibit with posters, special artifacts, music, and food. The parents take pride in sharing their cultural heritages with their children's classmates, and they typically stand alongside their children at the booths. One of the school's few Muslim students is in Jane's class, and Jane is concerned about how other parents might react to this student's display, which includes Islamic traditions and holidays.

Tim recognizes the growing diversity of the community, yet remains aware of the potential for lack of understanding or exposure to different cultures for some families. The school librarian, Allison, had just been chatting with Tim about her interest in collaborating to expand this second-grade project. To date, she has mostly supported this activity with library resources and lessons on using text tools. But she has more ideas about building critical thinking and inquiry into the unit. Tim sees a possible connection across this interest and Jane's concern, so in response to Jane's question, he invites Jane and Allison to talk over lunch.

TIM: I appreciate your concern and foresight, Jane, and I wondered if we might be able to pull in our librarian, Allison, with some ideas she was talking about recently.

ALLISON: I've been reading a lot about inquiry and how inquiry builds students' engagement and critical thinking skills. We can incorporate pieces of inquiry into things that you're already doing, like the countries and cultures unit.

JANE, SECOND-GRADE TEAM LEADER: Is inquiry when students all come up with their own questions to research? I'm not sure how that would work here.

ALLISON: You're right—inquiry can be a process where students construct their own questions to investigate. In the library, I like to see students show their learning through lots of different products that can take a while to develop. But you can also try an inquiry process that's more focused and short-term, and not a big huge research project. I was thinking that for this topic, it might be useful to share some conversation with the children about similarities and differences across all the different displays as they are completing their work, not just the display about Islam.

JANE: Well, we usually let the students walk around and check out each other's booths. Is that what you mean?

ALLISON: That's part of it—yes! I wonder if you might help them build some questions, and then use that walking-around time as a way to gather information to answer the questions. I can suggest some stories and poetry about cultures to help inspire their thinking, too.

JANE: I'm seeing this now . . . and so when the parents come, the kids could even share their questions again, to keep building on the conversation.

TIM: I like where this is going. It's a lot of the same content that students have done in the past, but with some deeper thinking. If it might be helpful, I could co-write a note to the parents to help them anticipate the children's questions, and maybe even follow up with them at home.

In this vignette, the principal, Tim, shows the kind of support for the library program that benefits all students and teachers. He demonstrates investment and action by talking with the librarian and teacher and offering to reach out to parents. The school librarian, Allison, employs the word "inquiry" to describe the learning that she wants to see in relation to the second graders' projects, and Tim recognizes that what she wants to do is a natural and relevant next step for this existing event. Students gain thinking skills by constructing questions, integrating new information into existing knowledge, and conversing with peers about the artifacts in the cultural displays. When librarians teach inquiry, they aim to offer experiences that emphasize enduring understanding and self-assessment, whether the inquiry is in the context of a big project or a lesson in a single class period. School librarians didn't invent inquiry, but they apply its principles as a distinct and complementary contribution to instruction from subject-area teachers. As a school leader, you are likely already invested in developing students' critical thinking and lifelong learning. This chapter will help explain how the library program can contribute to those outcomes.

The next section provides an overview of what inquiry means in the library context, including four key processes to start your school on a good path toward inquiry and student learning. The first two processes are for educators. One is what I call the "collaboration arc," the partnership and explicit or implicit agreement between teacher and librarian. The other process is a consideration of the inquiry-based characteristics of an assignment or learning experience. For students, two essential processes are developing questions and self-assessing. Following this discussion, I'll demonstrate how these four processes come together in some examples of library inquiry lessons.

INQUIRY OVERVIEW

Inquiry includes familiar steps of student research: breaking down a topic, evaluating and attributing sources, reading and comparing information from different authors, and synthesizing ideas. Inquiry in today's school library, however, might be considered a value-added version of research, where the cross-curricular connections, transliteracy, and communities of learners (the three conceptual bridges from chapter 1) amplify library learning to the benefit of wider student learning priorities. For instance, inquiry in a middle school social studies unit on ancient worlds might take the form of students presenting digital stories on topics that require close reading and extend their textbook learning. As part of a first-grade science unit on "the rotting log" (as described to me by first-grade teacher Adele Flynn), students develop research questions about insects, arthropods, and other creatures, and report what they find in a VoiceThread, an online narrated slide show that they share with parents.[1] Working toward a schoolwide culture of inquiry is a holistic goal that addresses existing and unfolding school priorities, not only objectives of a library program.

Today's inquiry is more than an updated name for research or the insertion of technology tools into familiar processes. Inquiry entails deeper thought, intention, and reflection than we may have asked of our students in previous iterations of research. According to Kuhlthau and colleagues, "Inquiry is a way of learning that prepares students to think for themselves, make thoughtful decisions, develop areas of expertise, and learn throughout their lives."[2]

Inquiry is a constructivist-based process of learning and a way of thinking. Library researcher, educator, and leader Barbara Stripling, citing educational philosopher and reformer John Dewey's progressive view, explains two significant principles of this approach to instruction (emphasis added):

> Constructivism seems to be a natural, and long overdue, extension of John Dewey's philosophy that meaningful learning emerges from a *series of experiences that have continuity* (they are connected to one another and to future experiences) and interaction (they are designed according to the needs and capacities of the learners, and the *meaning is derived by the learners as they reflect on and organize the ideas that emerged from the experience*).[3]

This statement sets up perfectly the intended outcomes of library integration in a school. (For a discussion of using specific models of inquiry at the school level, see the sidebar "Inquiry and Research Models.") The school library program fosters continuity when students are taught cumulative information and thinking skills across grade levels and subject areas. The meaning and reflection described are generated through purposefully designed learning experiences that require and model metacognition. Put simply, "Inquiry is an approach to learning that involves students in finding and using a variety of sources of information and ideas to increase their understanding of a specific area of the curriculum."[4]

In this way, inquiry has a lifelong learning dimension that echoes and in many ways complements the long-term goals of reading and writing instruction. For example, a first-grade reading lesson has focused learning objectives related to particular vocabulary or comprehension. The ultimate goal, though, is to link reading experiences so that primary-grade students become intermediate students, middle schoolers, high schoolers, and adults with literacy skills that translate and deepen and enrich lives long after any singular experience with a text. With a similar, long-range series of cumulative learning at its heart, inquiry aims for learners to engage with ideas around them and within them. Inquiry does involve specific steps and processes, but

Inquiry and Research Models

This sidebar provides a basic overview of three commonly used inquiry and research models for consideration and possible adoption by your school. For in-depth discussions of inquiry and research models, see the resources listed in note 5.[5]

Some schools integrate research models into library and research instruction as part of a school- or systemwide adoption of one model, in the same manner that a consistent style manual may be applied to student writing. The core steps are fairly similar: define a problem or question, establish background knowledge and a course of action, identify and evaluate sources, interact with and use the information, synthesize or construct something to share the learning, and reflect on the research. By following a consistent approach to teaching inquiry, students have opportunities to revisit the same process and philosophy of inquiry across many learning experiences.

If you are interested in adopting a research model for your school, discuss with your librarian and teachers what qualities of a model are important to them, and what they want to do with the model. For example, librarians may be interested in using a model within their fixed-schedule library classes and with teachers when they collaborate on student inquiry. Rather than introducing every research project as a brand-new process, a consistent model allows librarians to point to familiar steps from other projects, such as constructing a question or locating sources, and connect those steps with new subject content.

Stripling Model of Inquiry

Barbara Stripling's inquiry model is a six-phase model designed for recursive navigation. The stages are Connect, Wonder, Investigate, Construct, Express, and Reflect. Stripling distinguishes inquiry models from information problem-solving models based on inquiry models' emphasis on open-endedness and on students' thinking about process.[6] As Stripling describes the model, "The schema is actually a spiral because each inquiry experience should lead to new understandings and new questions and, therefore, new inquiry."[7] An integration of Stripling's model and technology tools is described later in this chapter.

Guided Inquiry

The Guided Inquiry process was developed by Carol Kuhlthau, Leslie Maniotes, and Ann Caspari. Its eight phases are "based in the model of the thoughts, feelings, and actions in Kuhlthau's studies of the information search process (ISP) of students."[8] Each of the phases of Open, Immerse, Explore, Identify, Gather, Create, Share, and Evaluate is designed around multiple "sessions" (not lessons) with a learner-centered starter, work time, and a reflection facilitated by a team guiding the instruction.[9] Three-member core teams plus an extended team of experts are recommended for implementing guided inquiry: "The third member joining the school librarian and the subject-area teacher may be a second classroom teacher, or a specialist in reading, special needs, technology, or the arts."[10]

Information Literacy Model: "The Big6"

The Big6 model was developed by Michael Eisenberg and Robert Berkowitz, and as the name suggests, it includes six steps for information problem solving: Task Definition, Information Seeking Strategies, Location and Access, Use of Information, Synthesis, and Evaluation. The Super3 is a simplified version for younger students, with these steps: Beginning—Plan; Middle—Do; End—Review.[11] In my experience, some librarians who work with primary grade levels don't use that separate model, preferring instead to use the same Big6, with adjustments as needed.

The authors describe the Big6 as "an information literacy curriculum, an information problem-solving process, and a set of skills which provide a strategy for effectively and efficiently meeting information needs. The Big6 Skills approach can be used whenever students are in a situation, academic or personal, which requires information to solve a problem, make a decision or complete a task."[12]

not with "answers" to a question as a finite objective or endpoint. The thinking is as much the goal as any finished product. The next sections examine how teachers, librarians, and students use inquiry to help students build that continuity, meaning, and reflection.

FOR EDUCATORS: COLLABORATION ARC

The "collaboration arc" is the term I use to describe the cycle of interactions between classroom teachers and librarians as they work to integrate their respective content. For the classroom teacher, the content is the curriculum of science, social studies, ELA, or other subjects, possibly more than one at a time. From the librarian's perspective, the content is a cumulative set of inquiry, transliteracy, and information skills practiced by students across library learning experiences. Like a narrative arc in a story, the collaboration arc follows a familiar, but potentially varied path from project to project. There are common elements of planning objectives and learning activities, teaching and co-teaching, assessing student learning, and reflecting on learning and instruction. There is variation in the intensity of collaboration from teacher to teacher, as well as between the same teacher and librarian on different projects. Not every collaborative inquiry project will have teachers and librarians mapping out every step and executing them together, and that's the beauty of the arc. It's bendable to the needs of the teachers and librarian.

Flexibility and room for growth in collaborative teaching are part of the arc, as well as the collaborative culture in the school. Doll emphasizes that although it may not be "possible to collaborate fully and completely with every teacher on every lesson . . . it is possible to incorporate a pattern of collaboration across the school, involving all teachers and all students."[13] I provide more discussion on the practical considerations for collaborations in chapter 7.

Montiel-Overall and Grimes explain in their longitudinal research study about science teachers and librarians collaborating for inquiry-based instruction that "teachers and librarians can be taught to be effective collaborators, and to use recommended innovative teaching strategies to improve content instruction, specifically inquiry-based science and information literacy instruction."[14] Having a collaborative partner through the steps of that arc supports risk taking and innovation. The openness and risk taking in having students construct and pursue questions is a conceptual commonality linking the mission of the school library program with discipline-specific thinking taught in subject areas like science and social studies, even the arts.

Besides the intellectual benefits for students when librarians and teachers collaborate, there is positive energy and motivation for the educators, too. Adele Flynn describes her school librarian's excitement as contagious: *What can I learn,* she wonders, when the librarian approaches her with an idea for a project or technology tool. *What new thing is she going to tell me?*[15] This is a common strength among school librarians: their knowledge and their disposition toward sharing with colleagues. That skill set is important in putting in place the elements of inquiry across the curriculum. Barbara Stripling describes inquiry as "a relationship between thinking skills and content," and explains that "the overall framework of inquiry is essentially the same for every content area, but the embedded process skills are applied in discipline-specific ways."[16] Librarians work with subject-area teachers to tailor inquiry experiences to the content, and to help students notice cohesion across skills applied in different classes.

FOR EDUCATORS: ASSIGNMENT DESIGN

Whether in a librarian-taught lesson or a collaborative research project co-taught with a classroom teacher, inquiry often implies moving away from assigning specific questions for students to answer with "correct," singular responses. Giving students a choice of research topic from a list used year to year (e.g., choose a country, person, era, conflict, animal, court case, religion, etc.) is a familiar and comfortable way for teachers to assign research. Students may even enjoy doing these reports, finding freedom in the opportunity to select an appealing topic and pleasure in the chance for independence in pursuing the steps of finding books or articles and piecing together a paper, slide show, or poster. However, this report style of reading and, frankly, regurgitating doesn't demand the rigor and value that we can offer students.

Loertscher and colleagues group these kinds of reports into the category of "bird units," a descriptor that school librarians may recognize from their book *Ban Those Bird Units*.[17] "Bird units" have become part of the vernacular of school librarians. A bird unit—essentially interchangeable with the country, biography, biome, invention, and so on unit—comes in two varieties, according to the book. First is the fill-in-the-blank worksheet, where students skim through texts or articles to locate piecemeal information. The other is the report/term paper, which can devolve into cutting and pasting.[18] This kind of report usually requires minimal practice in the thinking skills that classroom teachers would recognize from the upper range of Bloom's taxonomy. Thus, if you hear a librarian mention a bird unit, you're probably not hearing a compliment.

One of the major requirements in making the leap from bird units to inquiry is guiding students to construct (and later, pursue) good questions. As Loertscher et al. explain, "A good question will not be able to be answered by cutting and clipping answers from an information source. A student will not be able to find their work already done for them from some website or reference book."[19] One way to introduce question-asking is through inquiry-driven class discussions, woven into the curricular focus but with recognizable prompts and characteristics across topics and settings. Asking questions and paying close attention to students fosters personal connections and different ways of engaging with content introduced in classroom lessons, and it is also a demonstration in slowing down and being intentional. Attention to this formative stage of the project is an opportunity to guide students in talking about the ongoing learning, check in, and invite conversation about what students have done so far and what the next steps may be. In this way, educators model how and why we attend to the process, not only the product. We open up space for students to grasp a rationale for the learning and strategies to take into the next inquiry process.

Another benefit here is connecting the students in their shared but individual processes and introducing early on the idea that there will be differences among projects, as with the cultural projects in the opening vignette. As Jane, the classroom teacher, talks through the many ways of being a family, of celebrating traditions, and of representing heritage, she models for students good practices in listening to and understanding other perspectives. It takes encouragement and practice to affirm the idea that there is more than one way to interpret a topic, especially in classroom climates where it's more typical to aim for learning outcomes that look the same. Even if the process is gradual, the realization that it's OK to take an idea into new places plants seeds of creativity, which is a good foundation for the dispositions of inquiry.

Following this trend of differences among projects, a strategy gaining momentum in 1:1 learning settings and technology-focused instruction is allowing students a choice in applications and tools, rather than prescribing one tool for all. For example, in a seventh-grade study of local water quality, students might read a textbook selection together and take a field trip to learn about water testing procedures. Upon their return to school, a common follow-up activity might be a journal entry about this experience. With some help from the school librarian, students might deepen their learning experience by articulating an inquiry question before their field trip, and then choosing a format for responding to their question when they return to school. Some might elect the written journal form to reflect on their question, but they also might record a video, tweet to a legislator or scientist, post to a blog, or make a photo essay.

In this way, students have the agency to choose how they want to interact with texts and show their learning. There is some risk to this open-ended, what-might-happen inquiry stance, but such an approach addresses reality, too. First, as previously noted, teachers and librarians can't be experts in everything; they are the conductors of the symphony, the subject experts, guides, coaches, and mentors, but they can't play all the music themselves. Giving students the leeway to pursue an independently motivating thread of the content is practical. In addition, giving students this freedom also requires that they test ideas, problem-solve, and think creatively along the way. Choosing apps for finding or creating content can have teacher-established parameters, but even the choice of a few apps enhances differentiation among learners and adds a new layer of learning. Students must be intentional in articulating or perhaps exploring to figure out what they want a tool to do for them, and then they must attend to the process of finding the right tool for the task. Granting students this kind of experience garners diverse evidence of learning for assessment of process and assessment of product.

FOR STUDENTS: THINKING AND QUESTIONING

Critical thinking, which we might say is the heart of inquiry, is indeed "an intellectually disciplined process," according to Scriven and Paul.[20] It's more challenging to demand inquiry and questioning from students. With teachers "handing off" the learning for students' active construction, and not just passive reception, by design, more responsibility and engagement are required of the students. As educational philosopher Jennifer Mulnix explains, critical thinking is both a learned skill and a set of intellectual virtues characterized by the learner placing purpose in the application of reasoning skills, via "some sort of metacognitive awareness on the part of the thinker of her own thought process."[21] The AASL Standards for the 21st-Century Learner similarly emphasize thinking about one's process of learning through self-assessment and self-questioning, from assignment-specific questions (e.g., "Have I located resources with diverse perspectives?") to more transferable considerations, such as, "How will I get help to edit and revise my project?" The idea of constructing and adjusting a path is addressed by the potentially complex question, "What is my plan for research?" and queries that test for bias, such as, "Does this work give me a slanted picture of the world?"[22]

Finding a "Bad Article"

Another component of active thinking and self-questioning in inquiry is noticing when a course correction is needed, and then following through with a change. For example, in a high school world religion research project, librarians might teach students to recognize whether an article gives them the information that they thought it would. Here's what can happen: the research is under way, and for whatever reason—a misleading title, a change in direction, too many of the same kind of article—a student realizes that she has a "bad article." Asking good self-questions, like "How does this article support my thesis?" encourages active thinking and demonstrates that the research road may be bumpy. It can be an unsettling sensation to realize that something you selected (perhaps after significant effort) isn't so great. But, librarians teach students that it's not a failure that they selected this piece; it's a success that they noticed its shortcomings!

This is authentic, sophisticated evaluation of information, and a skill that is applied not only in viewing a list of search results but also in interacting with the information. Acting on that knowledge of the so-called bad article, perhaps better termed a mismatch, requires a shifting of gears, and a revisiting of steps in the research process. Students may have to change a search strategy or attend to the evaluation of the article in a different way, and find a better source. That's where the discipline part enters in. "Satisficing" (the term that library science applies to a search process that yields passable results) isn't enough to cut it.[23] Librarians help cultivate the persistence that good research demands.

FOR STUDENTS: DEVELOPING QUESTIONS

Inquiry places hefty demands on students' thinking, but in turn makes learning more personal, and ultimately (we hope) changes for the better how students interpret and interact with information in their everyday lives, beyond a particular assignment. In this section, we'll look at how developing inquiry questions makes for more personalized inquiry experiences for students.

Dialogue

Setting up a classroom dialogue with student-driven questions is an accessible way to build inquiry skills and practice skills in speaking, active listening, and self-assessment—skills that are often featured in library lessons, but don't have to stay in the library. A dialogue that promotes questions and self-reflections is the type of activity that can work across subject areas and teachers, and can be made more successful with a small but focused effort from school leaders to roll out the strategy. Use your librarian's expertise and your teachers' input to help you unite successful discussion techniques across the school and infuse them with inquiry.

To help students generate questions, consult the self-questions from *Standards for the 21st-Century Learner in Action* (one of the implementation guides for the standards). These examples are useful, specific, and applicable across grade levels and subject areas in helping students think about and "take charge of their learning."[24] Questions from this resource, such as, "How does the evidence I found help me form an opinion or support a thesis?" and "What decisions or conclusions have I drawn, and how are they supported by evidence?" have broad applications, such as instruction of literacy strategies centering on text-based evidence.

Asking "How can I get feedback on my final product to use in my next inquiry project?" or "How have I contributed to the learning of others?" situates the learning in a collaborative, social, and responsive context. "Why did the author create or produce this?" and "How does this compare to other things I've read or viewed?" are questions that call to mind previous learning and a big-picture view of information, stories, and texts.

School library experiences outside of lessons also reinforce questioning strategies that students are learning in the classroom. Peterson and Taylor recommend higher-order questioning as a way to get students to think more deeply about what they read and to engage in higher-order thinking when they respond to texts orally and in writing. Librarians might incorporate prompts suggested by Peterson and Taylor, such as "Please tell me more about that" or "What makes you think that?" when talking with students about books they are reading.[25] With practice in a low- or no-pressure situation, students gain confidence in sharing and supporting their thinking.

INQUIRY IN PRACTICE

Elements of inquiry can characterize the teaching and learning and growing that take place in the school library all the time as a part of, but not limited to, what many educators might think of as class research visits. This immersion in inquiry at the level that is happening in the best school libraries extends far beyond library-situated skills or term papers. In the rest of this chapter, I offer examples of how inquiry may take shape in the school library and throughout the school. In addition to the following sections, see table 4.1 for three more inquiry examples from my own experience as a middle school librarian, including my estimation of the collaborative planning requirements as basic, midlevel, or in-depth.

Example 1: Second-Grade Cultural Fair

The second-grade cultural fair described in the opening vignette is a big schoolwide family activity, but the inquiry component might start small, in the classroom, with a facilitated class discussion. Rather than sending all the work for the family and culture research home with a big reveal for the fair, the teachers and librarian might invite the sharing of works in progress. For example, they might have students bring in one artifact or photograph that they have found so far, then model for the children some questions and responses that dig into the culture and traditions represented by the piece. For instance, the librarian might share a photograph of a family quilt, handed down through generations and made from stitched-together swatches of baby blankets and infant clothes. For a second grader, it might be a leap to ask "What does this quilt represent?" right from the start, but if the story of the quilt is about ancestors immigrating to this country, then the adults might build to this big idea by asking things like: How did you get this quilt? Who owned it before you? What can you tell me about the material and how it is put together? They might follow with guided and independent practice in small groups.

A positive outcome about the open-endedness of inquiry in dialogue and projects is that it opens up space for students to interpret a topic for their lives. The cultural fair was a common yearly event at a school where I once taught. However, it's not hard to imagine circumstances where asking students to research their family histories may be difficult or sensitive, like with children who are adopted, who are refugees, who live in foster care, or whose families don't have information about their histories.

Example 2: Sixth-grade Novel, *Number the Stars*

As a middle school librarian, I helped a classroom teacher build a more inquiry-based activity to accompany a prereading exercise for sixth graders reading Lois Lowry's Holocaust-era novel, *Number the Stars.*[26] In previous years, the teacher had prepared for students a vocabulary list and some question-and-answer sheets to fill out to help them learn about the time period around World War II. This was mostly a cut-and-paste activity, and with this topic, more discourse was needed to prepare students for the events in the novel.

Table 4.1 Three levels of collaborative planning

Subject area	Content focus	Inquiry focus	Collaborative planning requirements
Grades 6–8 Social studies or science content	Reviewing key concepts from textbook chapters	Formulating, asking, and responding to open-ended questions	Basic
Grade 7 math	Real-life applications of math concepts like geometry	Evidence-based reading and viewing of STEM career-related articles and videos	Midlevel
Introductory French	Using past tense (I went, I visited, I saw); identifying cultural landmarks and daily customs in French-speaking countries	Discovering personal interests in sights and activities in French-speaking countries; using countries and cultures reference database to find information; note-taking and attributing sources	In-depth

Instead of the vocabulary sheet, we built a lesson plan focusing on primary source images from the time period. Using the National Holocaust Memorial website, students searched for photos in a time period specified by the teacher. They composed captions for the photos, and as students got into the reading of the novel, they compared the families in the story to the images they had studied from the online photo archive. Not only was this a good chance to try an inquiry-based experience, it turned out to be a more reasonable, meaningful, and age-appropriate way to prepare for this novel.

Example 3: High School Health

To build connections between physical education and healthy lifestyles, a common health assignment is for students to find a current article about a health or fitness trend and summarize the article, or perhaps evaluate it for bias. To amplify the personalization, inquiry level, and student creativity in this experience, librarians and teachers might open up formats for students' reading and work products. Critiquing blog posts with comments (either within the class or posted to the blog) acknowledges a popular and potentially controversial source of health information and provides practice in appropriate civil discourse online. To interest student athletes, a phys ed–related option for studying sports in the news might be a kinesiology analysis of a stop-motion photo series of an athlete, or a video op-ed about the use of instant replay in sports.

CONCLUSION: STEPS TOWARD INQUIRY

Not every inquiry experience must be an enormous endeavor, in the same way that reading doesn't require finishing a whole book and math doesn't mean learning an entire concept all at once. As AASL affirms, "Learners do not have to complete a full inquiry cycle to be engaged in inquiry-based learning."[27] You might consider schoolwide inquiry as an opportunity to be economical, timewise. As we've started to establish already, setting the stage for inquiry can mean being intentional in crafting moments for students to strengthen questioning skills and curiosity. With some coordination from teacher leaders and curriculum leaders, educators can identify and maximize day-to-day moments that infuse inquiry. In other words, do things you do anyway with an inquiry orientation. School library educator Pam Berger writes of technology tools and inquiry:

> Times have changed; using Web 2.0 tools, these same students can collaboratively locate, evaluate, and share relevant Web-based resources

> using a social bookmarking Web site. They can post, edit, and share their findings on a class wiki incorporating links to videos, photographs, podcasts, and other online resources for their teachers, classmates, and others to view and offer feedback. They can collaborate with peers, manage and organize information, work in teams, and learn real-life skills.[28]

To help librarians and teachers channel the array of applications, Berger maps out the use of technology tools with stages of Barbara Stripling's inquiry model—Connect, Wonder, Investigate, Construct, Express, and Reflect—and teaching and learning strategies. For example, in the Wonder phase, where students are developing questions and making predictions, class brainstorming and peer questioning can be represented using concept map applications, where students input text into graphics and move around bubbles or boxes to help construct their thinking.

Bring together your teachers, technology coaches, and librarians to talk about and strategize how to maximize student thinking through technology. An elementary school librarian I know has an admirable and most practical philosophy for learning technology tools, and this might serve as a good place for your discussions to begin. She suggests that educators concentrate on just one or two tools, and think carefully about how the tools can support the component parts of critical thinking: questioning, self-assessment and metacognition, and construction of knowledge. With this concerted effort toward inquiry, students will not only develop the skills of inquiry that librarians aim to teach, but they will also prepare for the research tasks of standardized tests, graduation projects, and real-life problems that require adept information seeking and use.

CHAPTER 5

Assessment for Learning

Partnering with Teachers and Students

Assessing Process in Fourth-Grade Social Studies Inquiry

Michael is a fourth-grade teacher, and Julia is the school librarian at a K–5 elementary building. They are sitting down for the first time to bring together ideas and documents that they've each prepared for an upcoming collaborative unit on state history. With limited time for these face-to-face meetings, most of their planning has taken place through e-mail, and they've each been working on different tasks to share in person today. The concept is an inquiry project on the topic of human geography, which is part of the "home state" unit in the social studies curriculum.

Students will build inquiry questions that relate to place, and then work to answer their questions. This individual inquiry approach is a departure from the topical reports that Michael's classes have done in previous years on landforms and bodies of water. With this project, he will ask the students to think about physical geographical features, like rivers, lakes, mountains, and valleys, and consider how and why the bridges, dams, highways, and other human-made features of the surrounding landscape came to be. In the classroom, the students will learn about how people have used, changed, or worked with the land over time to address needs like housing, transportation, and energy. The students will choose one feature for their individual project and build a question that leads an inquiry into why that "thing"—a port, farm, or tunnel—"is where it is." The fourth graders will work with the librarian and use library resources to find information on their questions.

Michael and Julia are still working out the best ways for students to show evidence of their learning, as well as deciding how to structure the teaching time with the two of them leading the class together. Here, we pick up their planning conversation.

MICHAEL: So I think I have the learning objectives pretty well set. The kids always do a nice job with these reports, but I want to make sure that we really hit the text-based evidence piece of the standards this year. I like the idea that you described in your e-mail, about having them use images that make a great statement about "place." I started thinking about having the students use some kind of log to write down their sources as they use them, so they can keep track of the best points that make the case for the images they chose. What do you think?

JULIA: I like this! I wonder if we could add a process piece? It helps me to know how they are using the sources to find the information. For instance, say they look up "river" in the index of a book, and it gives them three or four page numbers with references to rivers. Can they check those pages and use the text tools to figure out which pages will help them with their question? If they have the structure of a log to guide them, they might pay closer attention to the steps of using the index, finding the selection that a topic points to, and interacting with the information.

MICHAEL: OK. That's breaking it down more than I originally planned, but I can see where you're going. I can review how they're doing with the content, check that they're on the right track, and if need be, remind them of topics we went over in the classroom.

JULIA: This sounds like a good self-assessment tool. When I've made these before, I've tried to think through what I need to know about their process after each day of work, and consider what that looks like. I wonder if a flowchart—like a big box that describes what they did and where they found information, then an arrow, and another big box for the next step, and so on—would capture what we need? They wouldn't have to fill it out for every lead that they follow, but even one or two would give us an idea of what they're trying.

MICHAEL: And give their parents some idea, too. The students will have an experience and a document to help answer "what did you do at school today?" I'll mention it in the newsletter that week, and ask the families to have their child talk them through the steps.

ASSESSMENT OVERVIEW

In today's climate of accountability in education, assessment is a chief concern of all educators. I believe, though, that there are opportunities for better clarity and communication about the assessment methods used by different educators at a school—including school librarians. In this chapter, I'll explain how assessment in the school library fits with inquiry and accountability for learning, and what principals should know and expect from school library assessment. Then I'll drill down into the librarian's assessment responsibilities, particularly in coteaching scenarios, using the opening vignette to illustrate what library assessment looks like. The chapter concludes with other assessment opportunities in the library and how principals can use assessment to find out the library's impact on student learning.

Harada and Yoshina offer this definition of assessment in *Assessing for Learning: Librarians and Teachers as Partners*:

> Assessment is the process of "collecting, analyzing, and reporting data" that informs both student and instructor of the progress and the problems that the student encounters throughout a learning experience. It differs from evaluation in that assessment is conducted as an ongoing activity that provides crucial formative information about what the student is learning and how that learning is taking place.[1]

The title's word choice of "assessing FOR learning," not "assessing OF learning," is significant for the library program's approach to assessment. The authors identify two underlying assumptions about "assessment as a learning tool that serves both instructor and student":

1. Students must be central partners in assessment.
2. Teachers must view assessment as integral and ongoing.[2]

These assumptions characterize the collaboration that I've envisioned between Michael and Julia, and the instruction that they are planning reflects these principles. First, students will be actively involved in the assessment because the knowledge gained from it is central to the whole purpose of the project—it is assessment, for learning. Next, for the teachers, the insights gained through assessment drive their instructional decisions. Ongoing assessment is critical to support the diverse learning paths and needs of students engaged in inquiry-based projects.

Assessment for learning has a fundamental intentionality that benefits school librarians and teachers working together. When a planning session involves careful breaking down of standards into experiences aimed at generating clear evidence of learning, teachers and librarians uncover and articulate the subject-specific goals, interests, and growth that each is working to realize with the students.

WHY LIBRARY ASSESSMENT SHOULD MATTER TO SCHOOL LEADERS

Many school principals don't readily associate the work of the school librarian with the role of assessment. Sometimes the teaching role itself is unexpected for principals and teachers, and sometimes "grading" and "assessment" are terms too readily interchanged. Grading library class can sound more tedious than beneficial. Assessment, on the other hand, provides evidence that the bridges between the library and school are producing results. School principals should expect their school librarians to be skilled in assessment to help them design and execute meaningful learning experiences aligned with the curriculum and standards. Sound assessment enables school librarians to give students instruction, reinforcement, and feedback on information, inquiry, and thinking skills within all subject areas. Librarians help students build independence and agility in using diverse literacies and thinking skills for subject-specific needs, and careful assessment helps them scaffold that process for students over time. The librarian has the chance to work with students year after year. Assessment is another positive outcome of that continuity, complementing the trust in, relationships with, and knowledge of students.

Preparing students effectively for the assessment of the Common Core State Standards is a focus for school leaders and teachers, including school librarians. Details of the standardized testing models for the CCSS are evolving and formalizing, with both state-specific iterations and those developed by consortia—for example, Smarter Balanced Assessment and the Partnership for Assessment of Readiness for College and Careers (PARCC) system. The research task component is a clear application of the inquiry and information skills that students develop through regular, varied library experiences involving inquiry, information seeking, and independent reading of literary and informational texts of different formats.

ASSESSMENT IN THE COLLABORATION ARC

In chapter 4, I introduced the "collaboration arc" to illustrate implementation of inquiry from the educator's perspective. Here, I use the same arc to present assessment in library-integrated instruction, first showing the planning, then the teaching and formative assessing, and finally the professional reflection.

Collaborative Assessment Planning

When a librarian and teacher collaborate and set up the big understandings that they want students to attain, they bring forward related yet distinct objectives. Michael and Julia worked backwards in their planning: they talked about what they wanted the students to able to know and do and what evidence each of them needed to see that learning.

Let's go back to the conversation between the librarian and teacher to highlight what each educator needs to know about the students' processes and products. Julia's expression, "interacting with the information," is a very "librarian" thing to say. For the current discussion, it is an instructive phrase for examining the library and information science expertise that she brings to this collaboration. A person outside the field of library and information science might not see that much to observe or assess in having students use books or online sources to get information for research. From an experienced librarian's point of view, however, such an exercise involves numerous decisions and actions. Thus, in her instructional role, Julia wants to be able to follow, assess, and support the students' pathways through that particular process.

When she enters this collaboration with Michael, she has the curriculum maps of social studies and ELA in mind, both horizontally and vertically. She can picture how the information skills in this lesson fit with the students' other work this year, as well as understand how the lesson is situated within the students' progression from third grade, to the current fourth-grade year, and ahead to the expectations for fifth grade. Julia wants to maximize her knowledge of the students, so she needs a teaching method and assessment strategy that allow her to provide key prompts that students will recognize. With the graphic organizer that they are planning to use, she can facilitate students' progress and hold them accountable for increasingly sophisticated skills. Plus, she can anticipate common mistakes or tendencies. To allow for this assessment, Julia and Michael structured the learning experiences to be purposeful, cumulative, and aimed at generating evidence of student learning throughout the project. In particular, they will gather evidence through the log and graphic organizer, and they will check in with students in personal conferences. Although they aren't including peer sharing in this particular assignment, it's a useful assessment strategy that school librarians teach. See the sidebar for more on peer sharing and review as a form of self-assessment.

Through formative assessment, Michael and Julia aim to enable students to progress toward big understandings and an eventual final product through benchmarks, feedback, and ongoing information and acknowledgment of the learning process. As Stiggins and Chappuis affirm, with assessment for learning, "students, not just adults, are data-driven instructional decision makers" and "everyone understands the definition of success from the outset and we generate an ongoing flow of descriptive feedback that permits students to watch themselves grow."[3]

Standards for the 21st-Century Learner in Action includes formative assessment as one of three levels of assessment for instruction in the school library; the others are diagnostic and summative. Michael and Julia's learning activities reflect mostly formative assessment, the work-in-progress perspective. In school library learning, formative assessments might take the shape of a tangible "thing," like the graphic organizer depicting the research steps, or it might be a face-to-face interaction, like an observation of a student's think-aloud through a sequence of actions in performing a database search. Michael and Julia don't mention diagnostic assessment in their conversation, although

Peer Sharing as Assessment

A factor that can make a task worth the effort for students is the expectation that parts of the work will be shared with peers. Learning how to give and receive feedback to and from peers is part of self-assessment as proposed in the AASL *Standards for the 21st-Century Learner*, whereby students "use interaction with and feedback from teachers and peers to guide [their] own inquiry process."[4] Students can grow in their own knowledge—on a variety of levels, not just content knowledge—by witnessing and engaging in the inquiry processes of their peers. Peers provide an honest audience and authentic context for improvement and reflection. As is the case with formative assessment, where students gradually learn to be receptive and find value in teacher feedback, accepting and giving peers comments, ratings, or ideas can take practice.

These are a few forms of peer interactions that support self-assessment:

- Exchanging of citations to check content or format
- Asking and answering questions about why a particular article or chapter was chosen
- Explaining how a website was determined to be reliable
- Pointing out the main idea of a paragraph
- Teaching a feature or troubleshooting a technology application
- Listening to or viewing a media segment
- Practicing dialogues, simulations, or speeches with a checklist for required components

they both bring evidence of this type of assessment to the lesson. Michael has been teaching the "place" unit in the students' social studies class, and through various measures like class discussions and quizzes, he has evidence to describe the students' "preexisting level of knowledge and skills, as well as their misconceptions."[5] Similarly, Julia taught the students' about self-assessment when using text tools in their library classes last year, so in her assessment, she monitors students' retention of these skills from the previous grade level.

Collaborative Instruction and Assessment

Harada and Yoshina's mention of "the progress and problems that students encounter" during learning is the type of information that Julia and Michael will collect and share with students and each other throughout the instruction.[6] If Julia and Michael were to conference with a student on why he chose his topic and what his beginning steps were in searching for information, they would each be attuned to different aspects of the learning. Julia would be interested to see if the student has narrowed down an inquiry topic, and has some ideas about the kind of information that will be useful in learning more about it. "How will you know you have found what you need unless you know what you're looking for?" is a mantra a librarian might repeat to her students.

As classroom teacher, Michael wants to find out if the student is following a topic that builds from and extends classroom activities about places as "locations having distinctive characteristics that give them meaning and distinguish them from other locations," as the standard dictates.[7] Michael would listen for how the student refers to the class discussion about rivers as geographic features that attracted early settlers, and how that made him think of a recent redevelopment effort on their city's riverfront. To make sure the student hits the major points of the standard, Michael would prompt him for key words and concepts, like how the riverfront has meaning that distinguishes it from other places.

The librarian's focus, meanwhile, would probably be gathering insights about the geography content that will help her monitor the student's choices of information sources from this point and how he uses them. She knows that students sometimes need help maintaining focus on the particular angle of the topic they are researching, and that sometimes an article doesn't turn out to be what the student originally thought. To support the affective dimension of research and the potential for frustration, she would intentionally use phrases like "getting started" and "trying this out" to acknowledge the possibility that the student might realize that a particular book or article doesn't offer what he expected.

She will also scaffold some self-questions. For example, "How does this article help you with your topic?" is a simple and effective question to ask the student directly, and one to encourage him to ask himself. Particularly with online searching, it's easy for students to be distracted by information that might sound useful, but doesn't really help answer the question. With the river redevelopment project, it might be helpful for the student to watch a local news story for any photographs, maps, or insights on the potential community impact. But it wouldn't be productive for the student to gather other related articles that might appear prominently atop a list of search results, such as bidding of construction projects, job fairs, retail and restaurant announcements, and other details that are beyond the scope of the task.

Julia's feedback and modeling of this self-question and other evaluation strategies (such as website reliability, checking currency and bias, or other checks) help the student decide if an information source is appropriate for the problem at hand. At elementary and middle school levels, librarians often narrow the field of options by suggesting particular reference databases or providing a curated collection of sources. Once students locate potential sources to address the need, Julia's focus will shift to how the students use a combination of text tools, reading strategies, and search functionalities to find the information within the book or article. This is the part that she will attend to when the students track their processes with the graphic organizer, while Michael utilizes the same graphic organizer to follow the student's exploration of the concept of place.

For reasons that include practicality, schedule, and the balance of the librarian's time with other classes, it's reasonable to expect that an entire inquiry project might not take place in the library, under the supervision of both the classroom teacher and librarian. But whether or not the final product is completed and unveiled within a "library lesson" doesn't mean that there isn't important information and feedback to be observed and shared along the students' process, to the benefit of the learners and the instructors. One more attribute pertaining to assessment that Julia brings to this collaboration is the students' trust in her, cultivated from working with her each year. This relationship strengthens Julia's capacity to guide the affective dimensions of the student research process. Students' receptiveness to constructive feedback—a crucial part of effective formative assessment—isn't automatic. Displaying persistence and emotional resilience in information tasks are dispositions to be modeled and discussed with students, including open, empathetic conversations about frustration and self-reflection.[8]

Concluding Projects and Reflecting on Student Assessment

Summative assessments help the librarian and teacher to discern whether the formative processes—the construction of a research question, the use of information sources, the understanding gained from self-assessment—were successful learning steps. There are several, loosely classified common categories of final inquiry or research products that librarians and teachers typically use as summative assessment. Papers are one, with the related staircase of components, such as note taking, paraphrasing, constructing and supporting an argument, and citing sources. Other written compositions fit in this category, including essays, narratives, stories or articles, poems or lyrics, and analyses and critiques. Another common form of summative assessment for inquiry and research is the presentation, with varying levels of face-to-face and digital components and purposes, such as debates, slide shows, digital stories, speeches, reports, and role-plays and simulations. Then there are the products of the makerspace or similarly imaginative opportunities for the arts, design, and engineering: inventions, solutions, programs and applications, and creative works. Sometimes the final product of an inquiry experience doesn't "happen" or go on display in the library, due to the realities of school schedules, and also because librarians and teachers are trying out new and different forms of content creation and sharing that don't necessarily lend well to a session of presentations and reporting out. This is why formative assessment can be so valuable for school librarians.

During my time as a librarian, I served as a state-level trainer for a series of school library professional development workshops called Assessment Planner and Assessment Product. One of my lasting impressions from facilitating the workshops to librarians in my region was the revelation and resulting discussion about how assessment and shared reflection were critical but often excluded parts of the collaborative cycle between teachers and librarians. In my mind's eye, I see Michael and Julia following through with the assessment together throughout the instruction and reflecting on it afterward to improve for next time, but like the librarians in my training session, I've been in situations where my teaching colleagues weren't on the same page when it came to the perfect picture of a collaboration.

"Assessing learning is an important factor, both for the students involved and for rating the effectiveness of the collaboration," writes Janice Gilmore-See. A strategy to help get collaborative partners on the same page, hopefully for subsequent projects, is exchanging honest, structured feedback after a project, even in the form of an online survey if there isn't time for a face-to-face meeting. I probably didn't do this enough as a school librarian. I could have learned more about my contributions with frank questions like, "What student learning was derived specifically from the expertise of the school librarian?" and "Could you (the classroom teacher) have done as well or better on your own?"[9]

As the librarian, it would have been helpful for me to reflect, and perhaps document over time, my colleagues' responses to questions like these: "Were you able to supply a missing component that the classroom teacher would not have been able to provide on his or her own or in the classroom?" and "Does the work product really highlight what the students learned and were able to do because of their library experience?"[10]

DESIGNING AND IMPLEMENTING MORE ASSESSMENTS

Some tasks worth doing may be the phases of a large inquiry project, and other tasks are of the "one-hit wonder" or "one-off" variety, perhaps co-taught by teacher and librarian as one lesson, or as a class led by a librarian teaching solo within a fixed schedule. Much of our discussion thus far has presented a picture of assessment in a collaborative partnership, but it should be noted that school librarians assess and contribute to schoolwide goals with solo instruction. What are some other ways that the school librarian might assess and provide feedback on student learning? Here, we examine librarians lending expertise to build assessment tools, assessment during a cycle-based library class, the use of library data for differentiated instruction, and forms of longitudinal assessment.

Analyzing Julia's interest in the student's research steps illuminates how her role in the planning and teaching is different from, yet dependent on, that of her classroom teacher colleague. When I was a practicing school librarian, I offered to contribute to assessment, sometimes to the surprise of my fellow teachers. For some teachers—not that I didn't offer it to all, some just preferred to grade and monitor students themselves—I helped make checklists for project components, reviewed drafts or logs of student papers or projects, co-designed and filled out rubrics and rating scales, and provided feedback or grades on students' final citations lists. The teachers weren't especially surprised that I was interested in gathering this information, but they were far more familiar with a model where the librarian was involved mostly at the start of a project, and then the teacher would oversee the rest of the student work and the grading. I suppose this is easier and in a way, more efficient than having to coordinate tasks or wait for pieces to be completed by another person. But fruitful collaboration for maximum student learning isn't just about the scheduling or "activity planning," and I think that's the part that we tend to leap to when envisioning a collaborative teaching endeavor. However, the teaching, assessing, and reflecting are also critical steps.

Library Class Check-Ins

It can be a challenge to both teach and allow time for checking out books, but there are creative ways to make it work. Some librarians use book checkout time as an opportunity to check in face-to-face with students on their reading choices or content understanding. If students are working on an independent learning activity, such as using an online catalog to find a book, taking notes from an article or media source, or writing a book review, the librarian might use a strategy like Chappuis's stars and stairs feedback. This assessment, "where the star is the success feedback and the stair is the intervention feedback," gives timely, manageable guidance for students so that they can see how they are doing and what to work on next. For older students, a similar assessment framework of "that's good, now this" might be used. Both systems "establish a forward-looking stance to corrective feedback: 'What's my next step? What do I need to do to accomplish this learning?'"[11]

Sometimes elementary librarians prepare a brief assessment of students to be performed during or after book checkout, such as, "Once you have your book, write the author's name on the whiteboard" (if they are learning about authors) or, "When you check out, tell Ms. Morris something that makes you interested in your book" (to build students' choice and identity as readers). One elementary librarian I know takes a quick video of a few students answering questions or telling her about something they learned. She reviews these later, takes note of areas of strength and need, and adjusts accordingly for future lessons. Some of my high school library colleagues and former students use online forms as exit tickets to check understanding or monitor progress.

In an elementary school where "specials" (e.g., library, art, music, physical education) are graded on a quarterly or semester basis, a student self-assessment of key benchmarks like preparation, active participation, and cooperation with classmates might be introduced. Daniel Pink suggests a DIY report card, where students devise and rate their own learning goals.[12] To complement the self-assessment, a steady routine of formative assessments through the grading term would reflect and guide instruction and learning in specific tasks, with feedback given as immediately as possible, delivered in ways that inform the teacher, librarian, student, and, as appropriate, parents and caregivers. The parent component in formative assessment is especially helpful when home-school connections might be drawn, like practicing tips for online safety, rereading or retelling a story, or using a graphic organizer to compare news reports from different points of view. In this way, the parent or caregiver can follow the child's progress with a more informed, current perspective than a periodic letter grade affords.

Collecting Library Data

Assistant superintendent Thomas Lesniewski offers an example of integrating data-collection-driven library programs and classroom instruction. During his tenure as middle school principal, the school librarian worked with language arts teachers to introduce an online reading comprehension and incentive program (Accelerated Reader) into daily classroom learning, as a way to promote and get students interested in reading choices, and to help students and teachers follow individual reading progress. To grant space and equipment for this purpose, Dr. Lesniewski facilitated the librarian's work with the district's technology department to secure a class set of laptop computers. They obtained unused tables and reconfigured part of the school library as a space for students to use the laptops for reading classes and other activities. The arrangement made the model of 1:1 devices available by class period more efficient. The computers were mobile, and hardwiring available at the tables supported access to charging and reduction in set-up and transition time from class to class.[13]

The school library program also gives school leaders opportunities to monitor progress of schoolwide initiatives through many of the systems already in place, including tracking student and class visits, analyzing usage statistics for articles and content on licensed reference databases, and viewing circulation of materials by curricular area via the library management software.

Longitudinal Assessment

Another aspect of assessment pertaining to inquiry is the study of information literacy progress at the school level on a longitudinal basis. For example, students' growth in information skills can be monitored before and after a learning experience (for a diagnostic and summative form of assessment), at different points during the year, or from year-to-year through such programs as the free TRAILS assessment tool. Developed by Kent State University Libraries, Tools for Real-Time Assessment of Information Literacy Skills is

> a knowledge assessment with multiple-choice questions targeting a variety of information literacy skills based on 3rd, 6th, 9th, and 12th grade standards. The assessment items are based on the American Association of School Librarians' *Standards for the 21st-Century Learner* and those from the Common Core State Standards Initiative that have been adopted by most states.[14]

Evidence for Librarian and Teacher Evaluation

Although my main focus in this chapter is assessment of student learning experiences, it's important to address some related topics of teacher and librarian evaluation. The TRAILS tool, used alone or alongside teacher/librarian-created assessments specific to the school, not only provides a picture of student progress, but also may provide data to track librarians' or teachers' goals (e.g., SMART goals: Specific, Measurable,

Attainable, Realistic, and Timely) established as part of teacher evaluation programs. Chapter 7 presents further discussion on collecting and applying student evidence within librarian and program evaluation.

WHAT ADMINISTRATORS CAN DO TO PROMOTE MEANINGFUL ASSESSMENT

As we saw in chapter 4, the process is as important as the finished product in learning activities focused on inquiry and the development of creative and critical thinking skills. The process of an inquiry-based investigation is where most of the information seeking, thinking, reading, and evaluating unfold, making assessment of process a chief concern for librarians. Assessment of inquiry processes may be a fruitful topic for discussion at grade-level meetings or a theme for librarian-facilitated webinars. To help identify more specific areas of interest and need, school leaders might incorporate assessment of inquiry and critical thinking processes into an action research cycle, wherein "individuals or collaborative teams can acknowledge concerns, generate improvement strategies, and assess outcomes to determine future actions."[15] Action research on inquiry may serve to foster ownership of this topic across the teachers and their priorities, making it less a "library thing" and more a "school thing."

What else can administrators do to promote successful, meaningful assessment for learning in the school library? Two strategies are meeting with librarians and saying yes.

Communicating with Your Librarian

Library science educator and researcher Lesley Farmer asserts the importance of regular communication with principals:

> By regularly assessing the fruits of collaborative labor, TLs [teacher-librarians] can determine which efforts are effective and what underlying conditions need to be strengthened in order to optimize the effect of future initiatives. Most important, though, TLs need to communicate

these findings with principals and collaborate with them to improve the entire collaborative enterprise.[16]

Best practices for communicating with school leaders is a popular topic within professional development for librarians. (I've presented on it myself!) In your position as school leader, asking questions of your school librarian opens the dialogue and demonstrates value for the librarian's teaching role.

In a statewide research study in Pennsylvania surveying the value placed by school administrators on key library practices and the instructional impact of the school library in teaching academic standards, "librarians were most likely to get 'Excellent' ratings from administrators who consider it essential to address librarian-teacher collaboration in teacher evaluation," which "suggests that when collaboration with the librarian is something on which teachers are evaluated individually, it is more likely to happen and produce positive results."[17]

In this study, most administrators thought that meeting with school librarians was a good thing, with nearly 96 percent of respondents deeming meeting with their librarians as Essential (23.6%), Highly Desirable (38.2%), or Desirable (33.9%).[18] Looking at subgroups of administrators who gave "Excellent" ratings for their librarians' teaching of standards in different content areas, 67.7 percent of administrators who gave "Excellent" ratings for their librarians' teaching of standards in ELA and 52 percent of those who gave the "Excellent" rating for teaching standards in reading/writing in history/social studies rated regular principal-and-librarian meetings as "Essential."[19]

The study findings suggest that an area for concentrated improvement might be the 34 percent of administrators in this study (and others sharing this mind-set) who rated meetings with librarians as Desirable. There are subtle nuances between the categories of Essential, Highly Desirable, and Desirable. To me, Desirable connotes interaction that is positive and helpful if it organically materializes, but not necessarily something so motivating that the administrator actively takes steps to initiate the meeting. Principals must make it a priority for the meetings to happen, rather than simply be satisfied with meetings if they do occur.

Meeting is a good thing! If you think that your librarian is already doing the kind of assessment discussed in this chapter, asking questions and sharing information will help to forge the next steps, maybe to extend the collaborative teaching to different teachers, or to brainstorm new ideas for linking particular student needs with effective assessments. If you aren't observing the kinds of assessment that elevate library instruction and co-teaching to measurable, well-aligned evidence of student learning, then you absolutely need to meet with the librarian. Ask about what assessment looks like now. Share the examples of formative and summative assessments that I've provided here. Show your interest and support for making the library a vital and quantifiable contributor to growth at your school.

High school principal Dr. Jesse Turner wants to know what's happening in the makerspace, hackerspace, and studios of his school's library. His librarians count on his authority in the school to carry out their vision of a nontraditional learning space, and with his welcoming stance on idea generation, they "don't do anything without scheduling a meeting," as he puts it.[20]

Saying Yes

Throughout this book, I have identified rationales and strategies for teacher collaborations with the school librarian to construct student learning experiences, including assessment components, that teach standards in ways that foster deep understanding and creativity, require an array of literacy and information skills, incorporate diverse resources, and support transfer of knowledge across contexts. The role of the school leader in allowing these collaborations to ignite and flourish might be as simple, yet no less powerful, as saying yes.

One of my favorite moments from my interviews with school leaders was how elementary principal Kendra King expressed what she does to help new ideas grow: "Say yes." A combination of trust (the outcome of careful relationship building) and legwork (including getting buy-in from teachers and seeking input from stakeholders) is required, King explains, to make ideas happen, even in the face of major barriers. When a loss of funding challenged the development of the new makerspace at her school's library, King, the school librarian, and teachers looked to their existing space and materials, and asked questions together. What do we have that we can change? Are there too many bookcases? What if we opened the blinds and made window seating? Can we re-cover furniture and brighten the space with paint? From these early steps, King recalls, the space and learning opportunities caught on. School principal Erik Burmeister concurs, in *Principal Leadership*:

> When a teacher is willing to try something new or wants to pilot a program that might serve students better, the response is always, how can we make it work?
>
> . . . we believe that attitude challenges us to find solutions where others might find dead ends; the effects can be seen in the large efforts of our school and the small decisions we make every day.[21]

These small decisions shape the school experience for learners. It is imperative that assessment for learning, not just for grades or scores or progress reports, is the guiding factor in the intentional, purposeful design of learning. In the article "Assignments Worth Doing," Jean Donham extends an instructional framework called "Authentic Intellectual Work" to library settings. These assignments are concept-based, situated in real-world applications, employ substantive technology integration, and foster active intellectual exploration. Donham explains, "Previous learning time is used to engage students in tasks worth doing—tasks that engage student intellects deeply, relate to real life, and challenge the 'principle of least effort.'"[22]

Michael and Julia's redesign of the landforms report has rich layers of learning appropriate for formative and summative assessments that serve not only "tasks worth doing," to employ Donham's phrasing, but also represent utility and transfer for student performance in standardized testing situations. This kind of assignment leaves space for creativity and individuality, while still remaining in concert with standards. School leaders can send an important message by showing interest in, guiding, and sharing this philosophy with teachers, and also with parents. As Michael noted in the opening vignette, substantive parent communication and suggestions for conversations at home are other benefits of the "paper trail" of formative assessment. The next chapter examines more family-school connections.

CHAPTER 6

Responding to Diverse Needs

Authentic Engagement with Families and Communities

Grants for Community Learning

Jodi is a third-year principal, and one of her goals for her supervisory evaluation is to apply for grant funding to support the district's literacy initiative. She just found a grant application that offers funding for programs to promote diversity and acceptance of differences, and she is wondering if a program sponsored by this grant might somehow fit her evaluation objective. She remembers that the school librarian, Jake, once offered to help teachers with grant ideas, so she approaches him at afternoon bus duty. Here is their conversation.

JODI: I'm thinking about applying for a grant that funds programs that support students' understanding and celebration of differences in families and cultures. I'm leaning toward some kind of reading program or event as a way to structure the proposal. I wondered if you might want to work with me. Do you have any suggestions for getting started?

JAKE: That sounds like a great idea! I've been thinking about expanding the students' options for reading clubs—we just have the afterschool paranormal club and the book bloggers now. Maybe a new group would reach some different kids.

JODI: That's exactly what I was hoping. I'll be honest—I'm aiming to earn a literacy grant to meet one of my administrator evaluation goals this year. But I think something related to accepting differences or building understanding across people is something we need right now, so maybe a reading program can address both areas.

JAKE: What about connecting with a community group, maybe the seniors or one of the business leaders' groups? We could do a book discussion, or maybe a series, and bring in some community members to add a different voice to the discussion with the kids. The students would have fun and learn a lot from some intergenerational connections. I can research some resources and tools. The grant funding could go toward the materials and maybe a lunch, and depending on the community group, we might even get some matching funding.

JODI: I like this direction! Do you want to plan a meeting to talk more? Maybe we could bring in the counselor and the ELA department chair. They may be able to help us tighten up the proposal and identify some possible target groups of students.

JAKE: Yes! Let's include the library student advisory group, definitely the counselor and teachers, and when we zone in on a community group, let's invite them in, too. We'll need to ask what they need, and what they're willing to do with us.

Jake and Jodi's interest in tying together school needs and the community through a school library program exemplifies the school library's potential as a source of cohesion and shared objectives across related interests in the school. School leaders can strengthen communication and involvement with students' families through the school library program. Moreover, school leaders can show the community at large that their schools, through the school library and other programs, serve and inspire students' needs for reading, creative opportunity, and media and technology.

This chapter examines the opportunities school libraries offer to empower and inform students' families, including shaping more effective experiences with homework, turning to families as an authentic audience for student work products, and supporting independent reading and information use at home. We'll also look at how the school library supports students and families of diverse backgrounds with materials and services. Finally, we'll widen the lens to consider how community connections can be made stronger through school library programming. We will explore how library outreach like the reading program discussed by Jodi and Jake can foster positive relationships across the school community.

SCHOOL LIBRARY CONNECTIONS TO STUDENTS' FAMILIES

As school leaders, you have many channels through which you connect with students' families: conferences about children's academic and behavioral needs, sports and extracurricular events, school board meetings, and day-to-day interactions. Students' families are often the best sources of information about their children's needs. Communicating with parents and caregivers about school libraries can provide school personnel with valuable perspectives on children's cultural backgrounds, their reading needs and habits, behavioral and emotional concerns, and interests. These insights enable librarians and teachers to provide individualized, responsive, and meaningful experiences with inquiry, information, and literacy. Let's look at how the library supports student learning from this exchange of information.

Making Homework More Focused Through Recommended Resources

Library resources collected and organized by the librarian and made available through the library portal or website can help student work done at home become more productive. A powerful way to utilize the school library to connect with students' families is through concerted efforts to provide home access to library materials for projects and also for personal reading and information. Explaining and promoting virtual library resources to families helps reinforce the use of quality, appropriate content for students. Parents are introduced to skills being learned in the classroom. The library website demonstrates the range of materials and guidance available to students through the school library.

Librarians can work with classroom teachers, parent-teacher organizations, and the school principal to communicate the availability and quality of library resources online and in the library. Some existing tools for getting the word out are school or class newsletters, parent meetings, school blogs, and in-school displays likely to be seen by parents visiting the school, perhaps in the lobby or office. Sharing online resources also provides an apt moment to offer strategies for using online information and social media responsibly and productively. Ethical and productive participation and commitment to digital citizenship are skills that lend easily to family and community involvement. Through school social media and websites, your school can model and talk directly about strategies for maximizing positive use of online tools.

A simple but effective virtual-library promotional strategy that teachers and librarians might introduce to parents for use at home is to set the school library website as the home page that students see when opening up an Internet browser. The goal is to bring to mind instruction from the librarian and teachers and point to resources developed specifically for assignments, such as a guide to useful articles, links to the class blog, or suggestions for applications for producing and organizing content. With some intentional web design (supported by the technology department) and guidance from teachers and school librarians, students may be more likely to integrate library resources and strategies into their search habits.

I like the idea of the library portal as home page for classroom computers, too. Prominent placement of a librarian- or teacher-mediated resource in front of students realistically addresses their Internet tendencies. They already know how to get to Google from the library website or any other Internet launch point. However, it might be less natural for students to jump onto a computer and type in the library website, unprompted, when facing the familiar and easy Google search bar. Putting the voice of the librarian in students' ears, so to speak, can serve as a helpful reminder to use databases, to review pathfinders, or to visit teacher-developed resources. If your school uses an online course management system as the communication portal for families, then you might consider placing a visible link to the library from the welcome screen, perhaps with a frequently updated message to catch the eye.

Suggesting Families Serve as Authentic Audiences

The products of student learning, especially projects of the digital variety, may surprise families. Parents tend to expect that the conclusion to a big assignment might be an oral report or written synopsis, or perhaps the sharing of a slide show or poster. As a different, possibly more impactful sharing of learning than the show-and-tell approach, why not invite families and others from the school community to view the products of student learning? If students anticipate a potential community response and impact, then they may see more clearly a purpose to their work.

At the secondary level, authentic audiences can introduce "spaces for students to openly question, challenge, and investigate social and cultural issues" within critical inquiry investigations.[1] We examined inquiry in chapter 4. Kafi Kumasi-Johnson takes inquiry a step further with critical inquiry, which "help[s] students understand relationships between power and domination underlying various information problems, and [helps] students develop creative ways to work toward social justice."[2]

Kumasi-Johnson suggests that critical inquiry introduces new empowering roles for students as true scholars, where "students become teachers who are capable of raising important questions and investigating real-life concerns, and in turn, educate their community."[3] Perhaps Jake and Jodi's book discussion from the opening vignette could incorporate a critical inquiry approach, or connect to an existing "one city, one book" event, which often reflects subjects meaningful to a community.

Supporting Independent Reading and Information Use

Another way for libraries to connect with families is giving parents tools and prompts to help demonstrate interest and assistance in students' independent reading. Librarians and teachers may share self-questioning and think-aloud strategies that caregivers can try with their children. With teachers and librarians already consulting to help students select appropriately challenging books and apply strategies, parents can add another dimension of encouragement, feedback, and investment in the literacy learning process.

Here are some more ideas for connecting with literacy learning at home: Have students use self-assessment tools that require students to share or teach part of a search technique or inquiry process at home. Encourage family reading nights. Host a book swap, where students bring books to exchange to diversify their home libraries. Provide a parent section of library resources online and in the print collection. Invite teachers to showcase student work through social media in order to share their learning with the community, be present in the digital spaces students and families frequent, and provide that audience for students' efforts.

ENGAGING FAMILIES FROM DIVERSE BACKGROUNDS

The nature of the school library program, with its emphasis on language, literacy, resources, and information, lends well to outreach to students' families. Look to your library program to contribute to your school's efforts in involving families in the school, responding to diverse needs, serving English language learners, and demonstrating culturally responsive practices.

Family Involvement

Sharing student achievements and efforts outward, from the school to families and community, isn't the only flow of information that community interactions should embody. It is equally important to afford opportunities for parents, families, and caregivers to introduce their needs, concerns, and contributions into the school and school library. By gathering feedback and inviting parents to contribute through surveys or advisory panels, or in volunteer capacities, school libraries can work to represent students' families, languages, and diversity in the library collection and outreach services.

A middle school principal told me that her school has a list of one hundred parent volunteers offering time to the school![4] I was surprised to hear about this level of engagement at the middle school level, where I assumed adolescents would probably rather not see their parents in the hallways of their school. But the school makes volunteering accessible and the opportunities varied, from library shelving help to assistance with occasional class projects, and parents respond.

Asking parents about their child's reading needs or their cultural background conveys the message that the home experience is valuable and important in a successful school experience. Showing this interest and openness is part of the relationship building in public relations, and part of the historical service orientation of libraries. I have taught graduate courses in storytelling for librarians, and one of our favorite historical librarian-storytellers is Pura Belpré, a children's librarian from Puerto Rico who became the first Puerto Rican librarian to work for the New York Public Library in the 1920s. She welcomed the children into the library for storytelling, and opened doors previously thought inaccessible to the Spanish-speaking families by offering Spanish-language materials and bilingual services.[5]

Through updated, rich collections, school libraries provide diversity of content not just in languages, but in experiences that children recognize or may soon encounter: families with same-sex parents, grandparents living with the children's parents in one household, foster and adoptive families, children and families who are refugees, and the many cultures and heritages of the community and world. Pura Belpré's work exemplifies a family literacy initiative, which is a more intensive effort of community engagement. According to the National Center for Family Literacy's definition, among the tenets of family literacy as "services that are of sufficient intensity in terms of hours and of sufficient duration, to make sustainable changes in a family" are parent-child interactive activities, parent training in literacy instruction and partnering with the child's educational program, literacy training for parents in order to enable "economic self-sufficiency," and a developmentally appropriate education for children.[6] Although Belpré's work grew out of the public library, school libraries can also lend support to family literacy programs, which may be facilitated by groups that include the public library and other family organizations.

Responsiveness to Diverse Needs

Working in collaboration with classroom teachers and students' families, school librarians can provide resources and services that make learning more meaningful for all students, including those who are English language learners and have limited English proficiency, as well as students with disabilities, mental health concerns, and behavioral needs. Some libraries offer a family resource center, with books and information, speakers and services, parenting support, and links to agencies and organizations.[7]

One of the most essential skills of a professional librarian is expert use of a range of tools for finding information for patrons, including students and families. This competency is less about "knowing everything" than having the content background knowledge and the professional search expertise to access information to support students' needs. It's impossible to predict what needs your students and families may carry, but librarians are trained to match people with information, and they are resourceful in doing it.

If you hear your librarian say something like, "I don't know, but let's find out," maybe with the follow-up promise that, "I'd be glad to help you get that information," you might be witnessing a couple of important interactions. First, you're observing an information professional help someone meet an information need. Most school librarians are teachers, as we've discussed, but they are also your in-house information specialists. Second, you may well be observing a student entrusting the librarian with his or her needs, whatever they may be: a combination of reading level, language, topic, and perspective. Feeling like the library "has something for me" and feeling comfortable enough to ask for it are important steps for students to practice and attain.

English Language Learners

For students who are English language learners, the school librarian can select materials and co-design learning activities that not only help with language differences (such as translated books or resources), but may also provide support for cultural differences that can make texts difficult for students to understand. Sandra Hughes-Hassell and Denise Agosto explain a critical need for support for students with limited English proficiency, who face "the doubly-demanding task of trying to interpret unfamiliar English words while trying to comprehend unfamiliar cultural elements."[8] Recognizing learning needs that relate to culture is a significant and growing pedagogical and instructional design focus for all K–12 educators.

You can use the library resources and the expertise of the librarian to help you and your teachers meet this need more effectively. For example, to support and welcome English language learners, school libraries might offer parent and grandparent nights in the library, illustrations and signage in multiple languages, and access to the librarian's expertise in selecting and facilitating use of technology equipment and applications that allow for reading along, recording and listening to audio and video, and accessing library materials in varied formats for language and literacy learning.[9]

Serving the needs of students with limited proficiency in English is a growing concern for school and community stakeholders as well. In a study of school library stakeholders in Pennsylvania, focus groups brought up the needs of English language learners. A consensus-building exercise revealed differing priorities pertaining to the most valued school library infrastructure. Focus group interviewees from urban areas "emphasized the school library as a center of information access for all learners, regardless of socioeconomic status, learners' ability, and English language facility." Participants from suburban areas identified the librarian's instructional partnering and technology leadership as valued infrastructure components. Researchers also reported that in asking participants what library-related topics they wanted to know more about, responses included learning more about information access for English language learners in the state.[10]

Cultural Responsiveness

The library's support of students' language-learning processes would ideally be situated within a schoolwide effort to be culturally responsive, which requires thoughtful leadership and reflection from librarians, teachers, and principals. Summers applies James Banks's four levels of multicultural curriculum as a way for librarians to gauge whether their library instruction, collection, and interactions with students are culturally responsive. At the most culturally responsive Level Four, the Social Action Stage, "Teacher-librarians team with colleagues and administrators to encourage parental and community participation in discussing issues that are critical to the community to build meaningfulness between home and school experiences."[11]

Summers suggests four ways for librarians to be proactive and model cultural responsiveness. These strategies build from and enrich the library's unique contributions to student learning that we have examined in the previous chapters.

1. Build trust in students, learn their names, and welcome the sharing of their cultural backgrounds in their reading and work.
2. Value cultural awareness, including one's own misjudgment; invite families into the school library; and go out into the community to observe and learn about students' cultures.
3. Foster motivation by focusing on students' strengths, asking students' preferences for being evaluated, and "develop[ing] a library connection that appeals to different cultures as personal relevance creates a more positive attitude towards school; a place that has not always been welcoming to the underserved populations because of their differences."
4. Establish inclusion by helping students get to know each other, and fostering an environment of good communication, respect, and connection.[12]

Cultural responsiveness also requires assessing one's own beliefs, biases, and expectations for communications with others. Cultural and family backgrounds may affect interactions in the library and at school, including how parents view assistance and their comfort with the English language in spoken or written forms.[13] Sensitivity to children's home lives was a concern when I worked with a group of graduate students who designed a geography lesson around having students identify their homes on a satellite map. I asked them to use their professional judgment in bringing the concept of students' homes into a whole-class activity, being mindful that some students are homeless, live in more than one home, or have a transient living situation, maybe as part of a military family or for other reasons. The mapping of homes was part of a community map project, and the graduate students talked about introducing more choices for the children's contributions to the map, in addition to mapping "home." They also widened the essential question for the lesson from "home" to "place," in order to incorporate human geography curriculum more thoroughly. By giving students the opportunity to map playgrounds, public libraries, school, and other familiar features, they deepened the content and addressed diverse student needs at the same time.

SCHOOL LIBRARIES AND THE BROADER COMMUNITY

I wrote this chapter's vignette as a vehicle for considering the range of people and outcomes that stand to contribute to and benefit from the school library program, including people and programs outside the school. This section looks at some possible benefits of a community outreach reading program.

The details of the opening vignette are based on real circumstances from my work as a school librarian. My principal frequently shared with me grant proposal ideas. He knew that I kept up with possible funding sources and that I had the pulse of ongoing happenings with our teachers and students. He also (quite accurately) predicted my enthusiasm for innovative new ideas that could potentially impact student learning. (See the sidebar "Local Professional Networks" to connect your school librarian to local networks like the ones I called upon for sharing best practices and professional opportunities.)

Local Professional Networks

As librarian, I turned to my professional network of local school librarians for professional growth and to follow programs in neighboring schools. The librarians within the county met quarterly for technology training facilitated by the intermediate unit, our regional educational technology and special services center, and once a semester for Saturday professional development offered through the local affiliate of the state school librarians' association. We learned about tools and resources such as streaming video, reference databases, and media production applications for recording podcasts. I shared what I learned at these sessions back at school through dialogue, mini-sessions, or more formal in-service workshops, demonstrating that as librarian, I was a dependable source for cultivating new ideas, and that the library was the place for implementing new tools and programs for our students.

Where I worked as school librarian in western Pennsylvania, the local network of school librarians was strong; most school librarians had completed their graduate degrees and certification from the same few universities with active alumni involvement. Through these channels, it was fairly easily to get to know and communicate with the school librarians across the region. We discussed everything from troubleshooting online library catalogs to student book clubs, volunteer programs, reading promotions, and collaborative lessons. Because most of us served as the only librarian for one school (or several buildings, in some cases), this network was highly important for sharing best practices and learning from one another. To help your librarian build these connections, ask him or her about local school library associations or LIS (library and information science/studies) university alumni groups. Perhaps consult with neighboring districts to discuss your librarians' participation in regional library professional development opportunities. Your librarians, teachers, and students will benefit from this avenue of community outreach.

As you're well aware, schools can be drivers of civic pride and unity, but unfortunately, schools can also spur significant dividing lines in a community. Boundaries tend to be harshly drawn over financial matters such as teacher salaries, funding of programs or facilities, and discussions of tax rates. It's important to remember that the same community members hearing information and forming opinions about the school are potential collaborators, stakeholders, and advocates for students. Whether or not residents have children in the schools, the choices of school boards and school administrators matter, and education becomes everybody's "business" in various ways. For school leaders and educators, it is a priority to communicate that the school has much to give to the community at large, not just for the future, but also for productive outcomes today. To build a fair and successful relationship with the community, and turn stakeholders into advocates, schools tell the community about the good things they do, and also follow and respond to community needs.

In many school systems, the communication of school events and news is handled through a public relations department, or staff designated as communication officers for the school. Public relations as a profession emphasizes the engagement of people, rather than the relaying of information. Since the field originated in the early twentieth century, "public relations has been defined in many different ways, the definition often evolving alongside public relations' changing roles and technological advances. The earliest definitions emphasized press agentry and publicity, while more modern definitions incorporate the concepts of 'engagement' and 'relationship building.'"[14]

We tend to think of the corporate context when hearing the term "PR," but the engagement and relationship-building components of public relations are a strong fit for the promise of partnerships and cooperation among schools, communities, and students' families. In the realized vision of Jodi and Jake's project in the opening vignette, students and community members will join together for book discussions and lunch, perhaps as the start of a longer-term relationship. With thoughtful planning involving the representative groups, this program can serve more than just lunch and a book talk. As with assessment in the previous chapter, making the purpose clear and open to all participants is also important for building community connections. Unlike ideas that come only from the school, the goals of a community program or partnership should be developed, communicated, and practiced together with all stakeholders, and that's what Jodi and Jake aim to do.

Reading and Reaching Out to Community Groups

During a school practicum visit one year, I observed a school librarian preparing for an event similar to this book discussion. At first, I thought it was a nice luncheon and a pleasant activity for seniors and students to share, but then I came to understand that the school library had actually become well recognized and appreciated in the town over many years for this lunchtime book discussion group. For this school, a positive image and residents who could speak to the advantages of a school library were a few of the many outcomes of the program. Let's look more closely at potential learning and community-building goals that Jake and Jodi might set for their program.

Academic Outcomes

The experience of reading and discussing the book contains numerous academic objectives, including the obvious decoding, comprehending, and meaning-making. In the group setting, reflection and self-assessment skills can grow, perhaps through guidance or inspiration from others in the group. When book discussion teams include adults, persons from different backgrounds or languages, or other individuals who aren't part of students' typical peer groups or family circles, then the exchange of perspectives can be eye-opening. From reading researchers Harvey and Goudvis: "When we apply our background knowledge as we read, we guide students to make connections between their experiences, their knowledge about the world, and the text they read. Connecting what readers know to new information is the core of learning and understanding."[15]

If Jodi and Jake's reading program were to incorporate intergenerational or cross-cultural conversation, they would likely collect a rich range of responses to questions like these, based on a "ReadWriteThink" strategy guide for making text connections:

- How does this story (or this character, this event) remind you of something in your life?
- How are events (or conversations, problems) in this story similar to things you have seen happen in the real world?
- How was (a particular event or interaction in the story) different from what you expected might happen, or different from your experiences growing up?[16]

This is the part of community programs where the observable outcomes interweave with results less tangible, but no less desirable. In practicing a dialogue-style discussion, for instance, students build skills in active listening, transitioning from one person's statement to contribute their own relevant points, and substantiating ideas with evidence.

I recently observed a seventh-grade class conduct an impressively sophisticated dialogue led by two students. What captivated me most about the conversation was the students' careful listening and bridging between their peers' ideas and their own, with mature and attentive phrases like "building off of what Joey said" or "thinking about that in another way . . . ." These are skills that align directly to academic standards in English language arts, which strongly emphasize students' skills in interacting with others. The Common Core State Standards give this portrait of a student who demonstrates independence in reading, writing, listening, speaking, and language: "Students are able independently to discern a speaker's key points, request clarification, and ask relevant questions. They build on others' ideas, articulate their own ideas, and confirm they have been understood."[17]

These performance qualities aren't just pertinent today; these are college and career readiness skills, too:

> To build a foundation for college and career readiness, students must have ample opportunities to take part in a variety of rich, structured conversations—as part of a whole class, in small groups, and with a partner. Being productive members of these conversations requires that students contribute accurate, relevant information; respond to and develop what others have said; make comparisons and contrasts; and analyze and synthesize a multitude of ideas in various domains.[18]

Demonstrating another instance of standards alignment (which Jake and Jodi might do to accentuate the academic drivers of their grant proposal), the AASL Standards for the 21st-Century Learner also call for students to make connections beyond the school setting, potentially outside students' existing experiences, to new real-life and real-world applications of learning. These standards are shown in table 6.1.

Community Outcomes

In addition to what we might call classroom outcomes, the students and community members gain a structured and supported opportunity to witness and gain respect for others' interpretations and questions, and perhaps to connect as neighbors through the stories behind one another's take on a book.

For young people, this kind of interaction with adults supports the growth of a different type of skills that I haven't mentioned yet: the Developmental Assets, a "set of skills, experiences, relationships, and behaviors that enable young people to develop into successful and contributing adults."[19] I introduce the Developmental Assets in my courses for children and young adult library resources and services to help preservice librarians understand the ways in which library programming can contribute to children's healthy social and emotional development.

Table 6.1 AASL Standards for the 21st-Century Learner, aligned with lunchtime book discussion event

AASL Standards for the 21st-Century Learner	Student learning activity in book discussion
AASL Standard 2: Draw conclusions, make informed decisions, apply knowledge to new situations, and create new knowledge 2.3.1 Connect understanding to the real world	Together with community participants, students draw connections between events in their reading and real-life events that they or the community partners have experienced.
AASL Standard 3: Share knowledge and participate ethically and productively as members of our democratic society 3.2.2 Show social responsibility by participating actively with others in learning situations and by contributing questions and ideas during group discussions 3.3.2 Respect the differing interests and experiences of others and seek a variety of viewpoints	Students and community partners model and practice active listening, relevant discussion responses, and construction of questions in dialogue with each other. The book discussion group presents new perspectives through sharing across age groups and possibly cultural backgrounds.

Source: American Association of School Librarians, *Standards for the 21st-Century Learner* (Chicago: ALA, 2007).

The Developmental Assets framework was produced by the Search Institute, an organization that conducts research and offers publications and programming designed around forty "research-based, positive qualities that influence young people's development, helping them become caring, responsible, and productive adults."[20]

Two examples of external assets potentially strengthened by the community book discussion project are the support offered by relationships with adults other than parents, and the empowerment that the community members extend to students in expressing that they value young people. Fostering students' Developmental Assets is a worthy reason to connect your school library (and the school at large) with the community. There is a balance in this scenario that serves as a useful reference for further conversations on this topic. The balance rests in designing an experience that supports student learning—as it should, as a school-based initiative—but also considers the needs and interests of the community members in the spirit of the public relations orientation, building relationships and engagement. Of course, one benefit of community partnerships is the chance to display the good things that schools do, and this is important. However, a community program may sustain even more far-reaching results by seeking feedback, assessing needs, and implementing adjustments in order to engage the interests of all the different participants: students, community members, and educators. It's this "engagement" that can keep the community conversation on a good track, across all kinds of communities: urban, rural, suburban, consolidated districts, and county schools.

What are other ways to engage with the community through student learning opportunities? The book discussion group is just one activity that may work for some schools and settings, but there are numerous other interests and needs that can be met by engaging with community members, including service learning clubs or events, government-sponsored programs or activities to introduce students to civics, business and organizational job shadowing and mentoring, and humanitarian or other community agencies, senior centers, and organizations in need of volunteers or participants in community events like charity races, clothing and food drives, or environmental efforts.

PUBLIC LIBRARY COLLABORATIONS

As noted earlier, family literacy can be a valuable collaboration focus for schools and public libraries. Public libraries share many desired outcomes and services with school libraries, including "knowledge of patrons and striving to meet developmental and individual needs, providing access to diverse materials and tools, building children's skills in evaluating and producing information and ideas, and fostering lifelong reading."[21]

Given those shared goals, another public library partnership to build, or perhaps revisit and update, is the summer reading program. Summer reading programs and required reading lists are a popular connection between the school and the public library, at varying levels of engagement and coordination. Summer reading programs help sustain and broaden students' reading skills and repertoires in the time away from school. However, as Pandora and Hayman describe in *Better Serving Teens Through School Library–Public Library Collaborations*, there is room for enhanced collaboration and planning among schools and public libraries in order to make summer reading programs motivating, engaging, and more impactful on student learning. They suggest timelines, meeting strategies, processes for selecting books and activities, and other collaborative opportunities to strengthen offerings for students through both educational settings.[22]

There are other kinds of library collaborations that can support student learning not only in the summer, but also throughout the school year and into students' lives beyond their K–12 years. Public libraries offer materials and technology to support students' independent reading and school projects, and in some states, public libraries and schools share access to the same consortia of subscription reference databases. Afterschool hours in public libraries are often a hub of student socialization, learning, reading, and technology exploration. Public library programming offers children and teens everything from traditional story hours and book clubs to chess and gaming tournaments; gardening, cooking, and crafting programs; and workshops on how to be a responsible babysitter or engineer a robot. Connecting students and their families to the many services and resources of the public library is another path to family literacy.

The transition to college and postsecondary learning settings is a topic of interest to high school and academic librarians, as the senior in May or June becomes a first-year college student in August or September. In either the high school or postsecondary setting, students need many of the same areas for instruction and learning pertaining to inquiry, evaluation and use of information, and expanding capabilities in content creation and curation. "Your" students are also the students and citizens of the public library and the community at large, and this connection is one to tap and maximize for powerful outcomes for the community and school.

CHAPTER 7

Practical Matters

Schedules, Technology, Evaluation, and More

AS YOU CONTEMPLATE the integration of the school library into your schoolwide vision of excellence in student learning, it is helpful to target some appropriate first steps. To help jump-start that process, I have developed a top ten list of quick things school leaders can do to start maximizing the student learning opportunities of their school library. Following this list, I suggest leadership and operations-related action steps related to library schedules and access, facilitation of teacher collaboration, and professional and program evaluation.

TOP TEN QUICK STEPS TO START MAXIMIZING YOUR SCHOOL LIBRARY

The list begins with perhaps the most crucial action of all: get yourself into the library.

1. *Walk into your school library.*
   What do you see? How are the spaces and seating arranged, and what learning activities are happening? How are students engaging with content, with one another, and with teachers? How are the adults interacting? Is the space quiet or are there voices? What

resources are available? What activities look like they fit well in the space? What might be less workable?

2. *Visit some other libraries.*
   Visit public libraries in your community and in other neighborhoods or cities. Visit an academic library, or the library at an institution such as a museum or research center. What activities are happening there? What resources are offered on their websites? What is the mission of the library? What services, spaces, or ideas might be brought back and shared with your librarian?
3. *Talk to your school librarian.*
   Talk about the library and school missions. How does he or she see the role of the librarian? Talk about the librarian's hopes for the space, the program, and the relationships he or she has or wants to build with teachers in the school. What are his or her interests for specialized professional development? What are the primary worries or concerns? What are your impressions of the library and its future growth? Talk about meeting together on a more frequent basis.
4. *Talk to students about the school library.*
   What do they like? What do they dislike? What do they need? Talk about simple things: lights, chairs, tables, book borrowing policies. Talk about bigger things: technology access, choice, diversity. What do they see as the best offerings of the school library, and why?
5. *Talk to teachers about the school library.*
   How do they interpret the role of the library? Do they use the library? How? What do they know about the library? What do they know about the expertise of the school librarian? Are they willing to model and talk about library integration for your faculty?
6. *Implement a schoolwide focus on self-assessment, starting with one or two questions.*
   Start, or continue with renewed energy, your students' thinking about thinking. Brainstorm a list of self-assessment, self-

questioning, and think-aloud questions with your teachers, and select a couple to try out for a designated period of time. Make self-assessment a common and easily understood word, even at the younger grade levels. Focus on one question for a month or week, such as, "How can I share this experience with others?"[1] Promote the question through daily announcements, the school and library websites, and class conversations.

7. *Together with your librarian, consider relaxing some library rules that open opportunities for access or collaboration.*
   Are you aware of the library's policies on class visits, technology use, and circulation? Do the teachers know about the policies? What are the reasons for the library rules and policies? Are the rules driven by the need for supervision, safety, sufficient materials for students, or past practice? If there are policies that don't directly support student learning, collaboration, and inquiry, consider new interpretations of policies for a trial period, and check back on their implementation and effectiveness. As Loertscher et al. describe, the learning commons creates a different first impression than more traditional labs and libraries. Here, "neither computers nor books get in the way. If we were to come back in an hour, we might see a completely different configuration of individuals and groups of youth, adults, or both, busily working, consulting, and collaborating."[2] That flexibility to open up spaces and allow for productive noise may be a welcome and effective change.
8. *Extend professional development opportunities to your librarian.*
   The ongoing implementation of the Common Core State Standards, the unveiling of research-based tasks in standardized testing, and the ever-changing information and technology landscape make for a busy professional development scene for school librarians. Professional development opportunities come in all forms: webinars, conferences, local and national professional learning networks, and organizational membership and committee work.

Encourage and celebrate these opportunities to add to the expertise of your school.

9. *Give the librarian the opportunity to lead professional development for your teachers and staff.*
   Invite your school librarian and collaborating teachers to share their successes and strategies for inquiry and information learning. You might even the keep the librarian as a standing agenda item for school faculty meetings. This is a great way to share even quick ideas and tips with the group at large, and to sustain the dialogue about inquiry, literacy, assessment, and a collaborative culture. Your librarian can also offer sessions on in-service days, webinars or flipped PD, and small-group instruction to grade-level or subject-area groups, or paraprofessionals.
10. *Go to a library conference or attend a professional webinar.*
   We are forced to acclimate quickly when we are thrown into the deep end, and sometimes this can be a very good thing. When you attend a school library conference, you can be assured that you will be welcomed and maybe even cheered for attending. In fact, some conferences offer reduced or free registration for school teams that include an administrator. This is for good reason. Librarians need principals' and other leaders' support and action to make the library the best it can be for students and the school. Stepping into the professional circles of the school librarian will give you a different perspective and new ideas to take back to school together.

Experiencing these ten quick steps will give you a solid footing in understanding the status of your school library and a range of reference points for guidance. I hope these activities inspire possibilities for your school, perhaps an evolving perspective on school libraries as a key component of learning, and even—like a good inquiry question should—new questions for you to follow.

What else do school leaders need to know and do to support a strong school library that enables student learning? When I describe best practices for school libraries, I always lead with student learning and quickly follow with collaboration between librarians and teachers. However, student learning through purposeful, innovative library-embedded experiences depends only in part on the skills and willingness of librarians and teachers. The inquiry, personalized learning environments, and transliteracy experiences that characterize today's school libraries are highly intertwined with the broader program of the library, which in turn relies on the operations and planning at both the school and district or system levels. In the remaining sections of this chapter, I examine the factors related to school leaders' support and action for their school libraries, starting with the elementary school library setup and then moving to elementary and secondary school library schedules within the school day.

ELEMENTARY SCHOOL LIBRARY SETUP

The K–5 or preK–5 library serves the widest age range of school libraries, and you'll likely see this reflected in the seating, shelving, and materials. Shelving in elementary school libraries is typically lower to allow students to reach books. Separate areas may be designated for picture books, easy readers and chapter books, and middle-grade novels and nonfiction books.

Sometimes elementary libraries have more than one instructional area to accommodate different ages, such as a story pit with leveled seating (similar to a small amphitheater) for younger children and tables for older children. Learning commons models, described in chapter 2, have shelves and tables on casters for easy rearranging. Most elementary school libraries have some desktop, laptop, and/or mobile device stations, docks, or carts that are used during classes or on an individual basis for searching the online card catalog, accessing reference databases, browsing the Internet, and using content curation and productivity applications. School space is often at a premium, and corners or workrooms within the elementary or secondary library double as space for specialists to work with students, for equipment and textbook storage, and as teacher workspace.

SCHOOL LIBRARY SCHEDULES

The goal of a well-planned library schedule is to ensure that the library program is offering equitable, balanced access to students. The examples of library collaborations and learning activities in this book represent a range of school library settings and schedules. This list presents an overview of common library schedules, followed by some discussion of striking a balance with a flexible schedule.

Elementary School Fixed Schedule

A fixed schedule is commonplace at the elementary level, including the school where I taught first grade. Students rotate through special classes that may include art, music, physical education, and library, usually once a week or as part of another day-to-day cycle. Often classroom teachers are assigned this time as a contractual prep period. A common schedule is six or seven library classes a day, usually with different grade levels. Not surprisingly, I've heard librarians refer to this as the revolving door schedule, where one class comes in as another is leaving, without a lot of time for working with students or teachers who aren't with the visiting classes.

Elementary School Flexible Schedule

The fully flexible schedule allows the librarian to schedule classes with teachers at any time, which allows for great flexibility in co-planning projects. With a flexible schedule, a librarian and teacher might plan for class visits several days in a row, or construct a lesson that begins with the librarian and teacher in the classroom and concludes in the library. Libraries with flexible schedules sometimes have independent book checkout available before and after school and during student lunch periods.

Elementary School Fixed-Flex Schedule

This schedule is exactly what is sounds like: a combination of fixed classes, say, 3.5 or 4.5 days a week, with blocks of time available for collaborating with teachers to plan or co-teach lessons, or host small groups in the library. This schedule presents a flexible balance of structured and open time. I recently spoke with a school librarian who had about four hours of flextime spread out in small blocks over several days in her schedule. The time is useful for more involved projects, especially when used in combination with the students' regularly scheduled library class. The incremental schedule does pose challenges for arranging collaborative teaching time across all classes of one grade level, however. For instance, the librarian and third-grade teachers may co-plan a unit with three 50- to 60-minute segments scheduled for student research, reading, and project development. In my experience, most student research projects require blocks of at least fifty minutes to allow for instructions, mini-lessons, and the varied research and reading steps that students follow. Most technology-embedded work requires transition time for logging into devices, accessing online tools, and shutting down. In 1:1 schools where I've observed, less time is required because students have their devices in hand. With varied, small blocks of flextime for collaborating, keeping all classes at about the same progress within their ongoing classroom units is practically impossible. With a more continuous block of time, projects can better follow the same pace from class to class.

I've also seen fixed-flex schedules that accommodate relatively free-moving independent learning, where students work in the classroom, library, or even the hallway, depending on their needs for materials or space. I once observed a series of lessons like this, where third and fourth graders started class in their technology classroom/computer lab, and then independently moved between the library and the classroom to find information in books, capture and upload photos, and seek help from the librarian and teacher.

Secondary School Flexible and "Mostly Flexible" Schedules

Middle school and high school libraries tend to operate on flexible schedules, wherein librarians and teachers work within an open library calendar to plan research and media production projects in the library or in classrooms. The middle and high school examples in this book reflect a flexible schedule. Some secondary-level librarians teach regular courses, such as research skills, as well as a range of special courses, including keyboarding, bully prevention, and speech communication. Creative use of flexible time allows for different ways of participating in the collaboration arc, by blending shared time together with asynchronous components, such as online lesson planning combined with face-to-face discussions.

I followed a mostly flexible schedule as a middle school librarian. The library calendar was largely open to schedule collaborations with teachers in the library or in their classrooms. In the case of the latter, I'd advise the classroom teachers not to send individual students to the library during those times. My contract-required prep period was covered in the library by another teacher who supervised individual students and sometimes checked out books. If I needed my prep period for collaborative teaching (if, for example, my prep was fourth period and I was co-teaching a class that met first, second, fourth, and sixth periods), I would skip or shift the prep period that day.

I had a few other teaching obligations on my plate: I co-taught the school's antibullying program, usually one class per grading period, per grade level. I taught these with the school counselor during social studies classes. In addition, for two years I was assigned a first-grade library class at another school near the end of the day. This posed a scheduling challenge: leaving during our school's last class period meant that sometimes I'd be available to co-teach all of a teacher's classes but one, and we would either avoid those days or make different plans so that I could work with that last class.

SCHEDULES THAT PROMOTE MAXIMUM STUDENT ACCESS AND LIBRARIAN INTERACTION

That flexible schedules allow for more collaboration and more integration of information skills into the content curricula is practically a mantra for school librarians. In order to co-teach, librarians and classroom teachers need common instructional time. A library program that operates exclusively on a rotational schedule—a scenario most likely to be found at the elementary level—doesn't allow for this shared time. Thinking about the collaboration arc, the planning and reflection components could feasibly be conducted electronically. But the central focus, the co-teaching, relies on the classroom teacher and school librarian being in the room together with students.

Flexible schedules must be implemented thoughtfully. A colleague recently explained what she observed and understood about the fixed and flexible schedules at her daughter's school. With a fixed schedule of library classes, where students visit the library for class and book borrowing on a regular basis, the children definitely had time and opportunity to get library books. But with a flexible schedule, she went on to describe, the students might or might not have a chance to get books. If her child's class wasn't scheduled for library time—whether for a collaborative lesson or simply to just get in and borrow books—then they might get library books on an inconsistent basis, or only when individual students asked for (and received) time to get books by themselves. I was shocked to hear this perspective on what I generally assumed to be an effective practice of school libraries. But this watered-down version of the flexible schedule didn't maximize students' time in the library. That's a problem. So how you do run a flexible schedule that allows for collaboration and co-teaching, and still supports independent reading? Let's start with the elementary level.

In a survey of Virginia and North Carolina elementary school libraries, researchers found that schools with totally flexible schedules showed more books borrowed (on average) as compared to schools with all other library schedule formats.[3] An effectively operating flexible schedule requires the leadership of the school librarian, who must reach out to classroom teachers to plan for book borrowing for independent reading, so that students read library materials not only as part of inquiry projects, but all the time. Book borrowing can take place when classes aren't using the library, with teachers and the librarian using online calendar tools to communicate openings and schedules efficiently and easily. Students might visit the library in the mornings, either freely or on a rotating schedule, or perhaps during lunch or bus pick-up, depending on your school's schedule.

There are some creative ways to plan a fixed elementary schedule so that teachers and librarians can coordinate their support of students' reading choices and progress. Perhaps on selected weeks of fixed or fixed-flex library classes, students visit the library during reading class for book borrowing, and the library class time is dedicated to a longer lesson. Or, to build continuity between classroom reading and library reading, librarians and teachers can construct a pre- or postlibrary mini-lesson, journal writing, or discussion.

At the secondary level, library supervision needs may restrict collaborative teaching or planning time between librarians and teachers, even when a flexible schedule might allow for time to meet. Librarians usually prefer not to "close the library" when they are co-teaching, but it becomes difficult or impossible to watch other students visiting from class, check out books for them, or answer their questions when teaching, especially if the teaching area is separated from bookshelves or seating. But getting kids into the library for book browsing, borrowing, and reading is paramount. So what can librarians do?

One strategy to maintain access to the space during instruction is to arrange for teacher coverage of students working or reading in the library if study period or other supervisory duties are part of your school's practice, which is what we did when I was a middle school librarian. Sometimes I enlisted the help of trained student volunteers to cover book circulation when I was teaching—they loved using the book scanner and took their job very seriously, so it was a viable alternative to interrupting a lesson to check out books. Some libraries set up self-checkout stations to allow students to sign out materials. We didn't have a book security system where I worked, but some schools use these to decrease theft or inadvertent "escape" of books, which may result from an unattended circulation desk. Sometimes I did "close" the library to independent student visits when I was teaching, with an explanation clearly posted.

ACCESS TO INFORMATION AND TECHNOLOGY TOOLS

Technology staff, administrators, and technology specialists may operate in the same sphere as the librarian, but with distinct roles. Librarians are sometimes called upon to act as technology support, often because of their knowledge and willingness to help, or because they are pressured to say yes. The focus of a librarian's work should be tasks that directly support student learning and teacher collaboration, and not troubleshooting technology. When possible, bring together the technology and library departments to coordinate resources, objectives, needs, and strategies for ensuring students have equitable access to library and technology resources at home and school.

A primary goal of such collaborations is to design and maintain a web presence that grants students the best access and pathways for using library resources and other tools online. Like the physical library space, the library website requires purposeful placement of materials and collaborative spaces in order to maximize utility and support learning needs and quality teaching. A good school library website has elements and a design that are inherently instructional, offering age-appropriate skill development and motivation for thinking, in addition to content. School library websites can incorporate instructional scaffolds for cognitive, metacognitive, procedural, and strategic processes.[4] Integrating the library website directly into instruction models the application of tools and builds familiarity with resources, priming students for independent learning after library or classroom instruction. Visit and review school library websites for ideas, and discuss with your librarian and technology team how to implement a website design that fits the needs of the school community. As Valenza found in her study of exemplary school library websites, librarian training in site design may be needed in order to make websites more "accessible and engaging" for students.[5]

A powerful approach for allowing a culture of information to permeate the school is to extend access to the library beyond the room and beyond the school day. As discussed in chapter 2, access is a key component of the learning commons. Address the scheduling side of the library with the librarian, teachers, and administrative team. For virtual access issues, work with your technology department to set up intuitive and quick access to the library website and catalog in the classroom computers and a shortcut or app on school mobile devices. Make student access as simple as possible, with easy-to-remember passwords for shared accounts, such as databases that require authentication outside of school. Establish an efficient process for reconsidering blocked websites, one that includes the instructional value of online materials and tools. Review your school's Internet acceptable use policy and social media policy, and reflect on their effectiveness for connecting students to tools that permit access to content creation, communication, and resources, while maintaining necessary security. See the sidebar "Modeling Digital Learning" for more thoughts on generating evidence of student learning through digital tools.

Tap the expertise of your technology department, librarian, and possibly your district's legal representation or solicitor to learn about student privacy and acceptable-use agreements with regard to online tools, particularly for students under age thirteen. This can be an opportunity to share goals and potential differences of perspective, not a hindrance to access. Consult the American Library Association for resources on access to school library materials, and discuss whether any of the following major barriers may be restricting access: "imposing age, grade-level, or reading-level restrictions on the use of resources; limiting the use of interlibrary loan and access to electronic information; charging fees for information in specific formats; requiring permission from parents or teachers; establishing restricted shelves or closed collections; and labeling."[6] Consider students' technology needs at home, and look to community businesses for financial support for technology initiatives or agreements for low-cost Internet service, as Superintendent Mark Edwards's district did in its rollout of 1:1 student laptops. At Mooresville, students in grades 4–12 have laptops, and laptop carts are used in K–3 classrooms. As Edwards recounts, the Mooresville Graded School District (NC) received financial support for technology infrastructure from Lowe's Home Improvement (headquartered in Mooresville), and Chamber of Commerce and Economic Development Commission representatives took part in planning meetings. A district education foundation offers financial support for required student technology maintenance fees ($50), and the local Internet service provider offers $16.99 per month Internet for families without access.[7]

Modeling Digital Learning

As Pam Berger recounted in a 2010 article, "A few years ago, students would search online in a few databases, type their research papers in Word, print them, and hand them to their teachers, perhaps sharing key points with classmates through a PowerPoint presentation."[8] This was a fairly familiar cycle of student research for some time. When presentation slides started to gain popularity as a format for class projects, I even had the occasional teacher whose assignments included both a slide presentation and a poster board, signifying to me that there was still uncertainty in relying on technology-based evidence of student learning. Although there is a level of skill required to produce different formats to display learning, like a slide show and a paper, today's technology tools allow for new ways of interacting with content and with other people, not only as a final product but as a process for learning.

Modeling and guiding teachers and students to purposeful integration of technology tools are skills that school leaders can cultivate in their school librarians. Using technology tools thoughtfully for curation, presentation, and conversation can be vital to the inquiry process. For this reason, nearly every state and national school library conference features sessions on integrating technology tools into inquiry and standards-based learning. AASL's "Top Websites for Teaching and Learning" and "Best Apps for Teaching and Learning" are national awards lists developed yearly to recognize the best online applications; their release each year is a cause for discussion and excitement among school librarians. Ask your school librarian to share these sites with teachers, and consider inviting teachers to become go-to experts on sites and applications that they especially like and use with students.

FACILITATING TEACHER COLLABORATION

There are many ways for school leaders to facilitate the integration of the school library into instruction across the curriculum, and taking steps to examine and support collaborative processes is essential. The depth and the ease of constructing collegial partnerships in meaningful ways depend on factors as varied as flexibility of school schedules, teachers' historical experiences and beliefs about cooperation and collaboration, and their familiarity with colleagues and especially curricula across grade levels and departments. Viewing the school librarian as co-teacher of the wider curriculum (beyond the "library" curriculum) may be a completely novel concept for you and your teachers. That this is a different way to interpret the library's place in the school, or the role of a "special teacher" in the instructional landscape, is an idea worth acknowledging.

In *Collaboration and the School Library Media Specialist*, Carol Doll explains types of barriers that might occur in efforts to collaborate. Conceptual barriers are those that reinforce "how things are done" in a particular school. Pragmatic barriers draw from schedules, logistics, or bureaucratic structures. Attitudinal barriers reflect teachers' and librarians' feelings about working together. Finally, professional barriers come from differences in training or exposure to collaboration models.[9] Doll recommends several strategies for librarians to overcome or minimize these barriers. She summarizes the strategies as four steps: "examine the situation; make sure everybody agrees about the outcome being sought; carefully plan and implement the instruction; and evaluate both the product and the process."[10] In the rest of this section, I draw school administrators into the steps of this plan.

To begin or recharge library collaboration at your school, you might talk with the staff about needs and concerns as part of the foundation for building schoolwide strategies for collaboration. Collaboration isn't always a pretty or appealing endeavor. Collaboration in service of the school's mission demands shared risk, responsibility, and accountability for student learning. The librarian should be a willing leader for your school, ready to initiate collaborations and offer learning opportunities even in the face of tough schedules and harried people. If this isn't a strength for the current librarian, then school leaders must take steps to secure mentoring, offer coaching, or provide professional development for that person. Student learning is riding on this critical function of the school library program.

Next, to put the ideas into action, be open, and encourage the librarian to be open, to different ways that collaborative planning and teaching might take shape, allowing for different forms and depths of collaboration to unfold. A good place to begin is to communicate that the librarian is ready and willing to provide co-teaching, co-planning, informal or formal professional development, and of course, rich resources for students and teachers. The librarian's reach in the school may be an existing and robust network of collaborators and co-teachers, who are already informing the librarian about curricular needs and seeking help, incorporating library resources into teaching, and planning and co-teaching lessons together with the librarian.

Or, perhaps your school has a librarian-to-teacher network in its infancy, with much potential for growth and maybe even more options for a school administrator to lend support. Here, the goal might be for the librarian to maximize the opportunities he or she has to work either directly or indirectly with as many teachers as possible. What might that look like in your building? You might include the librarian in communications about goal setting for departments or grade levels, or in committees for implementing new curricular programs, so as to initiate conversations linking the library to the classroom.

Last, consider taking risks that open opportunities for collaboration in the school through innovative management and operation adjustments, such as helping students and teachers make productive use of flexible library periods and planning time. In collaborations with (or even without) the librarian, the culture of collaboration is likely to be more successful with time for planning and reflection. How much time your school librarian has to plan with classroom teachers is one way to measure how a school library program measures up to the best programs. According to the *School Libraries Count!* survey, a longitudinal study conducted by the American Association of School Librarians, librarians in the 95th percentile of responding schools spend seven hours a week meeting with teachers to plan instructional units. Librarians in the 75th percentile spend three, and those in the 50th percentile spend one hour per week planning with teachers.[11]

In districts where librarians have technology help desk or help ticket duties (in which librarians receive electronic help requests via an automated system), administrators might consider replacing or reducing a librarian's tech support tasks with designated time for collaborating. Or, if tech instruction is a legitimate need, use the time and the librarian's professional expertise for helping teachers apply technology to student learning outcomes, and channel the more clerical help desk queries to trained student volunteers or paraprofessional staff. Demonstrate your support by taking and assessing risks like this, as well as by highlighting good work in newsletters or faculty meetings, by showing your appreciation through compliments and questions, and by visiting ongoing collaborative activities.

EVALUATING THE LIBRARY PROGRAM AND SCHOOL LIBRARIAN

Evaluation of the school librarian and school library programs are two separate, but related topics to broach with your librarian. The librarian can help you parse the criteria and goals to evaluate the person's performance (e.g., collaboration, student learning outcomes, professional development, and other contributions) and those components that align with evaluation and growth of the program (e.g., the collection and resources, access, class visits, services available to the school). In Shannon's study of administrators identified as supportive of school libraries, "Two-thirds of respondents indicated that working with a librarian (as an administrator or as a teacher) was the most important source of their knowledge of school library programs."[12] As Danielson explains, "Evaluator-teacher conversations, when conducted around a common understanding of good teaching—and around evidence of that teaching—offer a rich opportunity for professional dialogue and growth."[13]

Professional Evaluation

Be sure to conduct some background work together to determine how school librarians are classified for evaluation purposes in your district and state. Are they considered teachers or support staff? Or perhaps your district evaluates professionals like school librarians and counselors according to a specialized category that reflects split duties: some direct interaction and instruction with students, plus work in other administrative roles.

In a study of perceptions of school administrators who took an online course in school library advocacy for administrators, Levitov found that school administrators "acknowledged that the school librarian has a unique position and should be looked at differently when conducting appraisal and evaluation."[14] So what does that unique evaluation look like? If librarians are indeed evaluated as teachers, consider that school or state-mandated teacher evaluation tools may capture only part of the work done by the librarian. If possible, discuss and identify additional areas to track and support so that your librarian's contributions are reflected in the evaluative process. Some state school library organizations have created resources, such as collections of SMART (Specific, Measurable, Attainable, Realistic, Timely) goals and templates, that librarians can use to report work conducted in collection management, collaboration, and professional development for teachers.

Consider context-specific criteria for classroom teachers' evaluations when instruction is conducted in the library setting as part of a teacher/librarian collaboration. Are co-teaching pedagogies reflected? How are the schedule of the librarian and frequency of instruction considered when evaluating student growth? What does an area such as preparation for teaching require of the librarian, when tasks include developing the library collection and curating online content in addition to constructing lesson plans? Invite the librarian to communicate his or her perceptions on the strengths and potential weaknesses of the evaluation instrument for representing the work of the librarian, and consider (within parameters of the employee contract) ways to document evidence of the work that the instrument may not address. If your district uses an instrument such as the Framework for Teaching (from the Danielson group), its layered study of teaching affords you the opportunity to evaluate and talk about the range of activities that librarians conduct in their work.[15] For example, evaluating teachers' facilitation of student discussions is one component in the domain of Instruction. (The other three domains are Preparation for Teaching, Classroom Environment, and Professional Responsibilities.) For the student discussion component, performance indicators assess quality of questions, discussion techniques, and student participation.[16] The specificity and data provided by this type of evaluative tool work well in assessing the work of librarians, which encompasses a wide range of teaching scenarios and administrative tasks, across the five roles introduced in chapter 1.

Also discuss with your librarians and administrative colleagues the evidence of student learning that your librarian can gather to demonstrate and plan for professional growth. Think back to chapter 6—what are the assessment processes and products that resulted from library-embedded learning in your school? Identify student learning artifacts that demonstrate objectives attained through formative and summative assessments in the library, such as research logs, self-assessment checks, graphic organizers, and digital media products. You can collect artifacts from the librarian, too, including the templates for these student assessment processes, and discuss how they align (or could better align) with curricular outcomes, deep understanding, and other school goals. Ask your school librarian to share with you the program and evaluation guideline publications from AASL, including *A 21st-Century Approach to School Librarian Evaluation* and *A Planning Guide for Empowering Learners: With School Library Program Assessment Rubric*, which includes online tools for strategic planning.[17]

What if you have a librarian who is just starting out, or doesn't do the things discussed in this book? Or perhaps you have a person on the job who isn't certified or doesn't have the MLS or MLIS degree? Continuous learning doesn't have to mean travel to conferences; many school librarians depend on a professional learning network (PLN) sustained through social media, where weekly chats bring librarians and other educators together for stimulating discussions, even via tweets. Rather than expect a new librarian to collaborate with all teachers, or lead a schoolwide workshop right out of the gate, encourage attendance at grade-level meetings to work on focused collaborations, or invite him or her to give a quick update at the next faculty meeting. For credentials for professional licensure, encourage noncertified librarians (if that scenario is possible in your state) to consider programs for certification, many of which are available online. Universities may offer a licensure-only program for teachers currently holding elementary or secondary education certification.

Program Evaluation

Consider other sources of information to inform the evaluation of the program. With the librarian's input on what information to gather, seek feedback from teachers, students, and families on the library program. (This needn't happen all at once, as this would result in a significant amount of data. Establish timelines for collecting information from various stakeholders.) Analyze the results together, and develop goals that are appropriate for the person's performance, such as more professional development offerings or continued efforts to collaborate with subject-area teachers, as well as goals for program-level, or more operational, growth. The latter might include accommodations for scheduling concerns, funding for materials, and student access to unnecessarily restricted websites or online tools.

On the program side, collection development is one example of an area for evaluation. A data-driven approach for school administrators to implement is to work with the librarian, technology department, and your database and catalog vendors to access usage statistics for the collection and online resources. What materials are in use? What isn't being used but could benefit the curriculum, and therefore may need promoting and modeling with teachers and students? What is less used, and perhaps less relevant to the reading and curricular needs of students? These may be items to consider for discontinuing (for online services) or deselecting from the collection (for print materials).

For your library website, consult with the technology staff to measure website traffic and web analytics, like what pages were visited and for how long. Work with the librarian to match up in-house resources (such as pathfinders for class projects, library newsletters, class blogs, and teacher websites) with their use. Establish a baseline for time spent on these sites, and monitor over time.

IMPLEMENTING PRACTICAL STEPS TOWARD SCHOOL LIBRARY INTEGRATION

I hope that by reading this through the lens of your own school's needs, you will identify and take action on strategies to harness the school library program for the good of your school. Like school principals, school librarians are resourceful, dedicated people whose work doesn't happen in isolation. The library program serves the entire school community and functions as effectively as possible within that school infrastructure, from the mission, to the curriculum and schedule, to strategic planning.

Some school administrators with whom I spoke while writing this book described having librarians on committees for curriculum, technology, and course management system selection. Within the parameters of reasonable expectations for involvement (committee service can be demanding), committees can be a good way to bring your librarians into conversations and planning across departments and grade levels. This service to student learning is school library tradition, from the professional handbooks of the 1940s, which proclaimed the library program as a service agency, a teaching agency, a materials center, and reading center (all of which are still true), to the slogan of the 1998 Information Power school library standards ("student achievement is still the bottom line"), to today's standards of multiple literacies and dispositions.[18]

One of the school leaders I interviewed described a recent budget discussion in which school librarians' jobs "were never on the table," because their contributions were so valued by the school principals and teachers. This district's librarians have strong advocates for their work. Gaining this support is an ongoing and intentional process for today's school librarians, many of whom do face potential cuts to their hours or their positions. Even among librarians whose jobs are more secure, the librarian role as defined in a school or system may be challenged by clerical or technology support tasks, possibly because other positions were cut. A frequent topic related to school library staffing is cuts to positions for clerical aides, library secretaries, or other assistants. The tasks of the program administrator role of librarians are ongoing and relevant responsibilities. Librarians prioritize and organize this work in order to maximize face time with students as well as time for collaborating and teaching with classroom teachers, and ultimately to increase the impact they can exert on student learning.

The school library's position as a unit within a larger system requires regular involvement from school leaders in order to maximize its outcomes for students. Librarians and students need the buy-in and support of school leaders to put into practice the vision of successful, impactful school libraries. In the next and final chapter, we will reflect on the reasons for pursuing that vision.

CHAPTER 8

Excellence for Libraries, Excellence for Schools

School Libraries and Student Learning

IT SHOULD BE CLEAR by now that I think a strong school library has great potential to make learning, reading, and information personally relevant and important to students. I believe that librarians and libraries can enable teachers to make student learning and understanding rich and more impactful. It's true that I tend to place school libraries in the center of conversations about education. But interestingly, absent a common prompt or yes/no question, several of the administrators interviewed for this book also described the library as a focal point of their schools. Here are a few of these descriptions:[1]

> "The library should be the heartbeat of the school."
>
> —*Scott Bacon, Principal,*
> *Blue Valley High School, Kansas*

> "The library is the pulse of the high school."
>
> —*Justin Zona, Curriculum Director,*
> *Fairview School District, Pennsylvania*

> "The library is a hub to increase engagement."
>
> —*Jesse Turner, Principal,*
> *Monticello High School, Virginia*

> "I always wanted for the library to be the educational heart of the building."
>
> —*Thomas Lesniewski, Assistant Superintendent for 6–12 Curriculum and Instruction, East Stroudsberg Area School District, Pennsylvania*

From the first school principal with whom I spoke to the last, libraries were indeed conceptual centers of their schools. In these libraries, students and teachers learn and instruct in collaborative, innovative directions, perhaps in ways that they may not have imagined they ever would. Principal Jesse Turner refers to his school's library as an area for creating engagement in a nontraditional way, where math might take the form of musical notes and writing might be constructed through song lyrics.[2]

A quality school library is desirable for these school leaders, and as I discovered, school libraries can be desirable for potential homeowners, too. I recently browsed a home developers' website and was delighted to notice that the library and its online resources were mentioned in the two-sentence description of the school. How would you describe your school in two sentences? Does the library's role in student learning merit mention? Library programs depend on school leaders to help make and implement decisions that allow programs to be successful for students—and make them worthy of pride in the school community.

The preceding chapters have offered examples, stories, and rationales for building responsive and rigorous learning opportunities through an excellent school library program. In this concluding chapter, we revisit the three conceptual bridges introduced in chapter 1 to recap and reflect on the ways in which school library programs contribute meaningfully to the school community. Then we will consider how the library program can drive professional culture and community, and conclude with a culminating look at the alignment of priorities across school libraries and leaders.

BRIDGE 1 · *Libraries provide links across content areas to support interdisciplinary learning.*

In most schools, the librarian serves all students in the building, and sometimes students in several buildings. School librarians apply their interdisciplinary view of curriculum as they plan and facilitate student learning activities. With purposeful instruction, this circumstance offers stability in the academic lives of students and sets up a unique perspective for linking content and assessment across grade levels and subject areas.

School administrators work to align the school and state curricula and lead teachers to "engage all students" with practices that "are personalized to accommodate diverse learning styles, needs, interests, and levels of readiness."[3] Processes and materials for this individualized, differentiated instruction are bolstered by library-integrated instruction that utilizes virtual and physical library spaces and materials. Librarians provide cross-grade-level expertise through vertical and horizontal curriculum mapping, and they align resources through the process of collection mapping. School leaders might also help facilitate collection mapping—that is, cross-walking the library collection to standards and curriculum—to ensure that materials meet current school goals and needs.

In a Delphi-method study of school librarians' dispositions, Jones and Bush categorized a quality of the school library perspective as "transformative of intellectual character," which speaks to that continuity of instruction that school librarians maintain with students:

> The school librarian not only focuses on integrating content in the curriculum but also focuses on the learner, on guiding and influencing an openness to new ideas and ways of making meaning, of critical and creative thinking, of building on the knowledge of the student as learner throughout each developmental stage.[4]

Transforming "library visits" into cohesive literacy and inquiry experiences across all subjects and grade levels affords more integrated use of questioning strategies, consistent self-assessment guidance, and thoughtful assignment design that makes the best use of teachers' and librarians' expertise.

BRIDGE 2 *Libraries foster transliteracy skills across information sources and tasks.*

The school library program is the school leader in transliteracy experiences, including establishing consistent expectations for using technology responsibly and for purposes of deeper inquiry and content production. Capitalizing on students' affinity for technology devices, librarians help orient students to the context, opportunity, and thinking processes of applying transliteracy skills, a skill set that that students are less likely to acquire in their informal uses of technology.

One of the most important charges for school librarians is preparing students to use other libraries now, as children, and as they grow into adults. This ambition is part of the bigger picture of lifelong learning, a disposition and goal that shapes the daily work and often the passion of educators. By providing spaces that welcome questions and offer pathways to reading, learning, and social exchange, libraries perform a valuable, essential function for communities and organizations, particularly in the information and technology climate in which we live. This affinity for and trust in libraries can be strengthened by emphasizing the philosophy that the school library space and resources belong to all students and teachers collectively, and not to the librarian as an individual person.

BRIDGE 3 *Libraries build collaborative, accountable communities of learners.*

A defining characteristic of school libraries is the provision of a caring place where students can spend time, enjoy social or quiet spaces, and feel welcomed. Following the example set by my mentor in school library education, I guide my school library graduate students to avoid calling the library "my library" or referring to "my collection." With the semantic shift to "our library" or "the students' library space," we convey the message that the library is for all and is not the personal domain of the librarian. The librarian is a teacher who gets to know and interact with students every year that they attend that school, and in this role, he or she can initiate this message of shared ownership. As the school leader, you can help set this example for your students and teachers, too.

The library is a safe zone for differences, a place founded upon the freedom to read, and a place where access to information helps students understand their identities and notice or form bonds with other people—whether in stories, at the next table, or in the global community. Jami Jones writes about school libraries' and school librarians' roles in promoting resiliency in children, those "protective factors that buffer children from adversity." Jones developed a conceptual "Library Ladder of Resiliency" that includes the factors of mentoring, reading, problem solving, social skills, and hobbies and interests as school library outcomes and characteristics that build competence and resilience in students.[5]

Gail Munde extends the library's circle of safeness and support to include teachers, nothing that "school librarians speak and write frequently about the importance of the school library as a 'safe and welcoming' environment for students, but librarians have the same potential to establish themselves as safe contacts for teachers and other school personnel, and to extend the school library proper to others for whom relatedness is a motivator and reward."[6]

Through these safe spaces, bolstered by programs to prevent bullying and promote community, school leaders and teachers fulfill significant areas of need for your students, and for each other. In my experience as a school librarian collaborating with the school counselor on bullying prevention, I learned that one of the most common reasons for students' absences from school is fear of bullying. The school library can assume an active role in fostering a positive, safe school climate. Particularly at the secondary levels, the library is one of those school spaces where students may perceive unstructured time as an opportunity for less productive engagement: teasing, gossiping, or bullying. However, the school librarian has the opportunity to get to know and work with all students across grade levels, and is often a person who builds a caring, trusting relationship with children by listening to and supporting their information and reading needs.

It's a common truth, too, that the library tends to be a magnet for students in need. Library resources, programs, and clubs can offer students the reading windows and mirrors that calm, assure, or open their eyes. The library collection celebrates diversity. Resources can provide answers to questions outside the homework: questions about family, relationships, health, sexuality, and the world around them. The library philosophy urges social and civic responsibility. The chance to become a creator of content and owner of intellectual property gives students a legitimate reason to care about copyright and use of information. The library is at once a community and a space for independent thinking and growth.

In all these ways, the mission of the school library serves the mission of the school. As the heart of the school, the library brings the mission of the school into everyday conversation and practice. At the school where I taught first grade, the mission statement of the school was posted on every door. In elementary school, a lot of time is spent lining up at the door, waiting at the door, marching through the door. Thus, this was actually a very clever practice for bringing the mission into the rooms. Not every day, but occasionally, the mission would catch the eye of a student or parent, and a conversation would ignite. The ideals of lifelong learning, student achievement, citizenship, respect for one another, and readiness for global communities—common threads in school mission and vision statements—are quite visible in the activities of the school library, including those pursued by students and modeled by teachers.

LIBRARY ADVOCACY AS PART OF PROFESSIONAL CULTURE

Some might still consider librarians to be "people who have little adult-to-adult contact with other educators in the building."[7] Yet, in the Pennsylvania school library study mentioned previously, school "administrators placed their highest value on librarians who serve on key school committees, partner with teachers to design and teach units, offer professional development for teachers, and provide flexible access to the library."[8] In short, they felt librarians and leaders need each other to thrive. As Deborah Levitov found in a study of school administrators' perceptions after they took an online school library advocacy course, "These administrators revealed through their comments that they do care about the library media program and they want to see the actualization of their action plans. At the same time they suggest they cannot accomplish it alone—the library media specialist has to play an important role and the teachers have to buy into the plan."[9]

Nominating committee membership or granting a librarian's request to serve supports the professional culture of the school, and may help to ignite other contributions to the library program through increased visibility of the school librarian. Collaboration and innovation in a school library program can bring out the best in your students and teachers, and this is a uniting goal in education, whatever the individual concerns and strengths of your school community may be. "The neediest learners may benefit the most from trained librarians and quality library programs," note Kachel and Lance on the findings of the Pennsylvania school library study.[10] When school leaders make choices to build strong school library programs, then they are also improving their schools at large.

School library advocacy is perhaps the most pressing concern of school librarians and those invested and interested in this field. As I have talked about in this book, school librarianship is a job that is not always clearly understood by the public or even by educators. Sometimes outdated views of the school library don't reflect the positive impact it can have on children's academic success, their lasting reading skills and habits, and their ability to navigate and harness tools for productivity, information, communication, and innovation.

For the school library context, "advocacy" is defined as an "ongoing process of building partnerships so that others will act for and with you, turning passive support into educated action for the library program. It begins with a vision and a plan for a library program that is then matched to the agenda and priorities of stakeholders."[11] Advocacy is interwoven in every component of the work of the school librarian, and gaining teacher and community advocates is a significant part of this effort. School librarians explain the value of their programs through everyday actions, like the questions, ideas, strategies, and curricular connections demonstrated in the chapter-opening anecdotes in this book.

Lean on your librarian's established channels of communication to extend the school's presence in the community in ways that will drive interest and investment in the school and in student learning. To advocate for the library is, after all, to advocate for the school and student learning. Consider grants and funding opportunities that involve community members and organizations. The librarian can also be a great resource for seeking grants that connect to the school curriculum and the culture of the school. One grant that we were especially proud of at our middle school was co-written by the guidance counselor, assistant principal, and me, in my role as librarian. As part of our antibullying and "learning about our differences" programs, we received a small grant to fund a speaker and teacher of American Sign Language who presented programs for each grade level. This event helped introduce the student body to the language and culture of individuals who were deaf and hard of hearing, including students and parents at the school.

In *Activism and the School Librarian: Tools for Advocacy and Survival* and in other advocacy-related articles, presentations, and toolkits for school librarians, a central goal is to build support for the library in ways that motivate others to take action on behalf of the library for the benefit of students. The book emphasizes the word "activism" to describe this effort, driving home that the process is about taking action to do the best work for students. Advocates can be teachers and students' families as well as legislators and others who influence and make policy decisions about education.

CONCLUSION: SCHOOL LIBRARIES AND STUDENT LEARNING

I constructed table 8.1 to show that there are prominent threads common to the responsibilities of school administrators and the mission of school libraries. These immediate and important links between administrators and librarians suggest parallel priorities and schoolwide interests. Through networks not all that dissimilar from principals', librarians are educators whose reach and influence extends across the students and teachers in the entire building, into community organizations like the public library, and into professional learning communities. Therefore, librarians are professionals to rely on to execute a cohesive plan that connects student, professional, and system-level learning with one another and with learning goals.[12]

My colleagues who are practicing school librarians and faculty who teach school library education frequently write about gaining support of school leaders in the journals, blogs, and other professional forums of librarianship and education. Faced with school library closures and staff cuts, and a stream of questions from numerous sources about the need for school libraries (or any libraries), my colleagues cheered my decision to write this book, often replying with some version of "we need that!"

Table 8.1 Alignment of school administrator responsibilities and school library mission

	School administrator responsibilities			School library mission
Responsibilities, tasks, and missions	*Five key responsibilities of principals*[a]	*Improving student achievement requires that school leaders . . .*[b]	*According to the six Educational Leadership Policy Standards, education leaders promote the success of every student by . . .*[c]	*School librarians empower students to be critical thinkers, enthusiastic readers, skillful researchers, and ethical users of information by . . .*[d]
Common theme 1: Through collaboration among educators, build trust and work for a common vision of student success	Shaping a vision of academic success for all students, one based on high standards Creating a climate hospitable to education in order that safety, a cooperative spirit, and other foundations of fruitful interaction prevail	Establish and build trust with teachers, students, parents, and the community	Collaborating with faculty and community members, responding to diverse community interests and needs, and mobilizing community resources	Collaborating with educators and students to design and teach engaging learning experiences that meet individual needs

Common theme 2: Lead teachers to a schoolwide culture that promotes and sustains effective instruction for student learning	Improving instruction to enable teachers to teach at their best and students to learn to their utmost	Provide instructional guidance, including an aligned and enriched curriculum	Advocating, nurturing, and sustaining a school culture and instructional program conducive to student learning and staff professional growth Ensuring management of the organization, operation, and resources for a safe, efficient, and effective learning environment	Instructing students and assisting educators in using, evaluating, and producing information and ideas through active use of a broad range of appropriate tools, resources, and information technologies
Common theme 3: Facilitate fair access to and allocation of resources	Managing people, data, and processes to foster school improvement	Allocate resources (people, time, money, space) in relationship to priorities	Acting with integrity, fairness, and in an ethical manner	Providing access to materials in all formats, including up-to-date, high-quality, varied literature to develop and strengthen a love of reading

continued

Table 8.1 *continued*

Responsibilities, tasks, and missions	School administrator responsibilities			School library mission
	Five key responsibilities of principals[a]	*Improving student achievement requires that school leaders . . .*[b]	*According to the six Educational Leadership Policy Standards, education leaders promote the success of every student by . . .*[c]	*School librarians empower students to be critical thinkers, enthusiastic readers, skillful researchers, and ethical users of information by . . .*[d]
Common theme 4: Contribute to an evolving system that fosters improvement and responds to changing conditions	Managing people, data, and processes to foster school improvement	Read, interpret, and respect context (a school's demographic, historical, political, and cultural characteristics) Encourage the use of data and research Develop people	Understanding, responding to, and influencing the political, social, economic, legal, and cultural context	Providing students and staff with instruction and resources that reflect current information needs and anticipate changes in technology and education

Common theme 5: Provide leadership and support individuals' opportunities to contribute to the educational vision and goals of the school	Cultivating leadership in others so that teachers and other adults assume their parts in realizing the school vision	Focus on parent and community support and engagement Redesign or structure the school organization so that priorities are consistently addressed Distribute leadership and approach leadership as a collective responsibility for teachers and parents	Facilitating the development, articulation, implementation, and stewardship of a vision of learning that is shared and supported by all stakeholders Understanding, responding to, and influencing the political, social, economic, legal, and cultural context	Providing leadership in the total education program and advocating for strong school library media programs as essential to meeting local, state, and national education goals

a. The Wallace Foundation, "The Principal as Leader: An Overview" in *The School Principal as Leader: Guiding Schools to Better Teaching and Learning* (New York: Wallace Foundation, 2013), http://www.wallacefoundation.org/knowledge-center/school-leadership/effective-principal-leadership/Pages/overview-the-school-principal-as-leader.aspx.

b. James H. Lytle, "Where Is Leadership Heading?," *Phi Delta Kappan* 93, no. 8 (May 2012): 54–57.

c. Council of Chief State School Officers, "Educational Leadership Policy Standards: ISLLC 2008 as Adopted by the National Policy Board for Educational Administration" (Washington, DC: CCSSO, 2008), http://www.ccsso.org/Resources/Publications/Educational_Leadership_Policy_Standards_ISLLC_2008_as_Adopted_by_the_National_Policy_Board_for_Educational_Administration.html.

d. AASL, *Empowering Learners: Guidelines for School Library Media Programs* (Chicago: ALA, 2009).

The enthusiasm is nice to hear—but it's really the students who "need that"—they need action on the part of their school leaders to make their library a school priority. I believe that students have much to gain through effective school libraries, and through the teaching, caring, and outreach of teachers and librarians. Extending support to new ideas can be risky. Projects and programs may fail. Teachers, parents, school administrators, and even some librarians may not like or understand the direction proposed here. However, to realize the promise of school libraries' impact on the life and learning of today's students, I believe this is a risk worth taking, one with an array of benefits for school leaders, teachers, and, most critically, students. Your school librarian and school library are essential elements of attaining your school's vision for student learning success.

APPENDIX

School Library Checklist

This checklist will be helpful as you consider the strengths of your current library program and how it may be integrated most effectively at your school.

1. LIBRARIAN AND LIBRARY PERSONNEL

The professional(s) and support team in the library lead and facilitate student learning.

- ☐ Do you have a school librarian?
- ☐ Does the person work full time or part time?
- ☐ If the librarian works at multiple buildings, what day(s) is he or she at your school?
- ☐ Is the person certified or licensed according to your state's requirements?[1]
- ☐ Does the person have a master's degree (the entry-level degree for school librarianship)?
- ☐ Does the library have a paraprofessional or volunteers?
- ☐ What are their tasks and schedules?

This information, along with the next set of questions on scheduling, will help you to consider when the librarian can teach, co-teach, plan with teachers, and administer the library program.

2. SCHEDULE

Library schedules enable but sometimes limit optimum use of the library.

- ☐ How is the schedule structured in your school library?
- ☐ Are there regularly scheduled classes in the library? If so, what percentage of the school day or week is scheduled for classes?
- ☐ Is there flexible time available for groups to come to the library, or for the librarian to visit classrooms?
- ☐ What is the process for arranging for instruction during flexible time?
- ☐ When may students visit the library independently?
- ☐ Are there set times for students to browse and borrow books?
- ☐ Is the library available to students before or after the school day, or during lunch?

You well know that school schedules can be highly complicated! Willingness to be creative with time and people, even within a tight schedule, can help ensure that students get library time.

3. PRINT AND ELECTRONIC RESOURCES

Together, the print and electronic materials in your library are the "collection." These are resources carefully evaluated and selected for your students and your curriculum.

- ☐ How many print volumes are in your library's collection?
- ☐ What is the average age of the print materials? Your librarian can help you get this information through the library catalog.
- ☐ Does the library have periodicals (magazines and newspapers)?
- ☐ Are subscription reference databases available for research?
- ☐ Where do the subscriptions come from? Many schools have databases provided via state or regional consortia, in addition to any that the school may purchase.

- ☐ What is the name of your library's catalog system for online searching for books and materials?
- ☐ Has the librarian been trained on this system, and has she or he trained the teachers?
- ☐ Can teachers and students access the online library catalog from classrooms and home?

The catalog is more than a way to find books on shelves. This resource is vital for connecting materials with your curriculum and student reading needs.

4. COLLECTION AND STUDENT NEEDS

The library collection is designed to provide appropriate resources for students' academic needs, free reading interests and abilities, and informational topics for student queries and questions.

- ☐ Is your collection mapped to the school curriculum? Librarians regularly build "collection maps" that demonstrate this alignment.
- ☐ Is the mapping current?
- ☐ What documents or resources show the alignment?
- ☐ What resources are available?
- ☐ What resources are needed?
- ☐ Do subject-area curriculum maps made by grade levels or departments reference specific library resources?
- ☐ How are library materials organized for student access?
- ☐ Is signage clear?
- ☐ Are books physically within students' reach and can they browse the shelves with ease?

It's helpful if shelves have some empty space for moving books around. Just like a sale rack of clothes so crowded that it's hard to see what's there, a bookshelf too packed with volumes doesn't allow students to pull out books to view and consider. A somewhat messy school library, with books on tables or not perfectly lined up on shelves, shows that kids are using the books. That's what you want! It's better to ease any fear of "messing things up" than to have impeccable shelves.

5. BUDGET

Library budgets vary widely in amount, structure, and procedures for designating and spending funds. Some libraries have a dedicated budget; others have funds that are grouped with other departments, such as ELA or technology.

- ☐ What is your school library's budget?
- ☐ How is the library budget situated in your school system (e.g., by individual school, by district)?
- ☐ Is there a specific line item in the school budget for library materials? This question is important, because a library budget is not a given. School librarians sometimes have no budget to purchase new or replacement materials because shared funds are diverted to other departments. School library resources are selected to support all students in the school, beyond the reach of what a department or classroom library can serve.
- ☐ If there is a budget for the library, who manages it (e.g., the librarian, a library department supervisor, other administrator)?

6. PROFESSIONAL DEVELOPMENT

The librarian is usually the only person at a school who functions in that capacity. Librarians' professional development needs are unique in that they balance two disciplines: library science and education. Time for professional growth with school colleagues is important, but so is training that relates to the library specialty.

- ☐ What is the professional development plan for your school librarian?
- ☐ Does he or she attend regional, state, or national school library conferences?
- ☐ Is he or she a member of state and national school library associations?
- ☐ Does the librarian offer professional development opportunities to teachers and school leaders (e.g., webinars, coaching)?

This balance of pursuing and giving professional development is a desirable leadership attribute of school librarians.

7. COMMUNICATION

Sharing information about activities and opportunities in the library is paramount to building connections to schoolwide programs and goals.

- ☐ How is information about the library shared with your teachers, students, families, and the community?
- ☐ Does the librarian regularly update the faculty at meetings? In speaking with librarians and principals for this book, librarians' contributions at faculty meetings ranged from a regular five- to ten-minute agenda item to one hour of a two-hour meeting for specific training.
- ☐ What calendars, newsletters, or other reports are offered to the school community?
- ☐ Are communication channels interactive? These might include online calendars, forms, tweets, or blogs.
- ☐ Does the library have a website?
- ☐ What resources are linked to the website?
- ☐ Is there student-created content on the website?
- ☐ Are library resources and classroom teacher websites linked?

- ☐ Does the library maintain a social media presence?
- ☐ How frequently is it updated?
- ☐ How is its impact or reach evaluated?

Find out the intended audience and evaluation process for sharing information with school stakeholders.

NOTES

Chapter 1

1. AASL, *Empowering Learners: Guidelines for School Library Media Programs* (Chicago: ALA, 2009): 50–52.

2. Ibid.

3. Contractual designation of the school librarian as a teacher or support staff may vary according to school system or statewide licensure/certification policies. It may be helpful to review this status with your school librarian to determine appropriate data to document for professional evaluation purposes.

4. Melissa P. Johnston, "School Librarian + Technology Specialist: Partnership for Effective Technology Integration," *Knowledge Quest* 42, no. 1 (September/October 2013): 70–75.

5. International Society for Technology in Education, "ISTE Standards Coaches," 2011, www.iste.org/standards.

6. AASL, *Empowering Learners*, 18.

7. AASL, *Standards for the 21st-Century Learner* (Chicago: ALA, 2007).

8. Ibid.

9. American Library Association. Presidential Committee on Information Literacy: Final Report. Chicago: ALA, 1989.

10. AASL, *Empowering Learners*, 23.

11. Technology in education will probably be a conversation topic for quite some time, but the language of technology is different for today's K–12 students and most of their teachers and parents. As Don Tapscott describes in *Grown Up Digital*, citing MIT epistemology professor Idit Harel, today's K–12 students (digital natives, individuals who were born in the modern era of digital technology) don't focus as much on the devices and applications as their parents and teachers do. For instance, if they shared a conversation on Google Hangouts or Facetime, they probably wouldn't emphasize the video aspect with the same air of novelty that digital immigrants (those born before current technology) typically would. In the same way that adults likely wouldn't make special mention of writing a note with a pencil, children don't typically distinguish that they are writing a story "on a computer." They just write a story. Don Tapscott, *Grown Up Digital* (New York: McGraw-Hill, 2009).

12. Debra E. Kachel et al., *School Library Research Summarized: A Graduate Class Project*, 2nd ed. (Mansfield, PA: Mansfield University, 2013), http://sl-it.mansfield.

edu/upload/MU-LibAdvoBklt2013.pdf; Audrey Church, *Leverage Your Library Program to Raise Test Scores: A Guide for Library Media Specialists, Principals, Teachers, and Parents* (Worthington, OH: Linworth, 2003); Frances Gretes, "School Library Impact Studies: A Review of Findings and Guide to Sources," August 2013, http://www.baltimorelibraryproject.org/wp-content/uploads/downloads/2013/09/Library-Impact-Studies.pdf.

13. Gary N. Hartzell, "Why Should Principals Support School Libraries?," *ERIC Digest* ED470034 (2002).

14. Kachel et al., *School Library Research Summarized*; Gretes, "School Library Impact Studies."

15. Church, *Leverage Your Library Program to Raise Test Scores*, 1–13.

16. Kachel et al., *School Library Research Summarized*; Gretes, "School Library Impact Studies; Church, *Leverage Your Library Program to Raise Test Scores.*

17. Briana Hovendick Francis, Keith Curry Lance, and Zeth Lietzau, *School Librarians Continue to Help Students Achieve Standards: The Third Colorado Study (2010)* (Denver: Colorado State Library, Library Research Service, 2010), ii.

18. Hartzell, "Why Should Principals Support School Libraries?"

19. PA School Library Project, "Creating 21st-Century Learners: A Report on Pennsylvania's Public School Libraries," 2012, 3, http://lgdata.s3-website-us-east-1.amazonaws.com/docs/2788/580001/Creating21stCenturyLearners_LibraryData Report.10.17.12.pdf.

20. Gary N. Hartzell, "The Multiple Dimensions of Principal Involvement," *School Libraries Worldwide* 8, no. 1 (January 2002): 44.

21. Carol A. Gordon, "The Culture of Inquiry in School Libraries," *School Libraries Worldwide* 16, no. 1 (January 2010): 85.

22. Bernie Trilling and Charles Fadel, *21st Century Skills: Learning for Life in Our Times* (San Francisco: Jossey-Bass, 2009), 117.

23. The Wallace Foundation, "The Principal as Leader: An Overview," in *The School Principal as Leader: Guiding Schools to Better Teaching and Learning* (New York: Wallace Foundation, 2013), http://www.wallacefoundation.org/knowledge-center/school-leadership/effective-principal-leadership/Pages/overview-the-school-principal-as-leader.aspx; James H. Lytle, "Where Is Leadership Heading?," *Phi Delta Kappan* 93, no. 8 (May 2012): 54–57; Council of Chief State School Officers, "Educational Leadership Policy Standards: ISLLC 2008 as Adopted by the National Policy Board for Educational Administration" (Washington, DC: CCSSO, 2008), www.ccsso.org/Resources/Publications/Educational_Leadership_Policy_Standards_ISLLC_2008_as_Adopted_by_the_National_Policy_Board_for_Educational_Administration.html.

24. AASL, "AASL Votes to Adopt the Professional Title School Librarian," *American Library Association*, January 16, 2010, http://www.ala.org/news/news/pressreleases2010/january2010/adopt_aasl.

25. AASL, *Empowering Learners.*

Chapter 2

1. Digital storytelling is a form of storytelling that uses media in concert with sequence, intention, and meaningful engagement to convey a narrative, often in a format open to participation from the audience. In this example, students facilitating digital storytelling with local senior citizens may have used recorded audio, photographs, and music to create digital stories. Brian Alexander, *The New Digital Storytelling: Creating Narratives with New Media* (Santa Barbara, CA: Praeger, 2011).

2. Maker Media, "What's a Makerspace?," *Makerspace.com*, 2014, www.makerspace.com.

3. Tony Wagner, *Creating Innovators: The Making of Young People Who Will Change the World* (New York: Scribner, 2012), 142.

4. Maker Media, *Makerspace Playbook: School Edition*, Spring 2013, 5.

5. Mega Subramaniam et al., "Reimagining the Role of School Libraries in STEM Education: Creating Hybrid Spaces for Exploration," *The Library Quarterly* 82, no. 2 (April 2012): 169–170.

6. Jesse Turner (principal, Monticello High School, Albemarle County Public Schools, VA), interview with author, February 21, 2014.

7. Fred M. Newmann, Walter G. Secada, and Gary G. Wehlage, *A Guide to Authentic Instruction and Assessment: Vision, Standards, and Scoring* (Madison: Wisconsin Center for Education Research, 1995), cited by Jean Donham, "Graduating Students Who Are Not Only Learned But Also Learners," *Teacher Librarian* 35, no. 1 (October 2007): 8–12.

8. Donham, "Graduating Students Who Are Not Only Learned But Also Learners," 12.

9. National Governors Association Center for Best Practices and Council of Chief State School Officers, "Common Core State Standards, English Language Arts Standards" (Washington, DC: National Governors Association Center for Best Practices, Council of Chief State School Officers, 2010), http://www.corestandards.org/the-standards/english-language-arts-standards/.

10. AASL, *Standards for the 21st-Century Learner* (Chicago: ALA, 2007).

11. David V. Loertscher, Carol Koechlin, and Esther Rosenfeld, *The Virtual Learning Commons* (Salt Lake City: Learning Commons Press, 2012), 1.

12. Gail Bush, "The Transliterate Learner," *School Library Monthly* 29, no. 1 (2012): 6.

13. Mark Edwards, *Every Child, Every Day* (New York: Pearson, 2014), 92.

14. Chad Stephenson and Jason Stone, "Why a Middle School Learning Commons?," *Teacher Librarian* 41, no. 5 (June 2014): 45–49.

15. Jennifer Reed (school library teacher, Newton Public Schools, Newton, MA), interview with author, July 30, 2014.

16. Joyce Kasman Valenza, "Curation," *School Library Monthly* 29, no. 1 (October 2012): 20–23.

17. Judy O'Connell, "Content Curation in Libraries," *Collected Magazine*, no. 6 (May 2012): 5.

18. Mary Madden et al., "Main Findings," *Teens and Technology 2013* (Pew Research Internet Project, March 13, 2013), http://www.pewinternet.org/2013/03/13/main-findings-5/.

19. Scott Bacon (principal, Blue Valley High School, Johnson County, KS), interview with author, February 2014.

20. Edwards, *Every Child, Every Day*, 89.

21. Jonathan Bergmann and Aaron Sams, "Why You Should Flip Your Classroom," chapter 3 in *Flip Your Classroom* (Alexandria, VA: ISTE/ASCD, 2012), 19–33.

22. Alliance for Excellent Education, "Expanding Education and Workforce Opportunities Through Digital Badges," August 28, 2013, 2, http://all4ed.org/reports-factsheets/expanding-education-and-workforce-opportunities-through-digital-badges/.

23. "About," Mozilla Open Badges, n.d., http://openbadges.org/about/.

24. Alliance for Excellent Education, "Expanding Education and Workforce Opportunities Through Digital Badges."

25. Shauna Masura, "Why Badges Matter for School Libraries," *Library Media Connection* 31, no. 1 (September 2012): 16.

26. Rebecca J. Morris, "Responses of Listener-Viewers in Digital Storytelling: Collaborations in the Intermediate Classroom and the Middle School Library" (PhD diss., University of Pittsburgh, 2011).

27. Kristin Fontichiaro et al., "Badging a Conference," *School Library Monthly* 29, no. 7 (April 2013): 5–7.

28. Shannon C. Hyman, "Planning and Creating a Library Learning Commons," *Teacher Librarian* 41, no. 3 (February 2014): 17.

29. Shannon Robinson, "Choice, Chances, & Changes," *Teacher Librarian* 40, no. 5 (June 2013): 25–32.

30. Jami Biles Jones, "Fostering Creativity Through Inquiry," in *The Creative Imperative: School Librarians and Teachers Cultivating Curiosity Together* (Denver: Libraries Unlimited, 2013), 187.

Chapter 3

1. Sherry Sanden, "Independent Reading: Perspectives and Practices of Highly Effective Teachers," *The Reading Teacher* 66, no. 3 (2012): 222–31, doi:10.1002/TRTR.01120.

2. National Governors Association Center for Best Practices, Council of Chief State School Officers, "Common Core State Standards, English Language Arts Standards" (Washington, DC: National Governors Association Center for Best Practices, Council of Chief State School Officers, 2010).

3. National Center for Literacy Education, *Remodeling Literacy Learning: Making Room for What Works* (Urbana, IL: National Council of Teachers of English, 2013).

4. Debra E. Kachel et al., *School Library Research Summarized: A Graduate Class Project*, 2nd ed. (Mansfield, PA: Mansfield University, 2013), http://sl-it.mansfield.edu/upload/MU-LibAdvoBklt2013.pdf; Debra E. Kachel and Keith Curry Lance, "Librarian Required: A New Study Shows That a Full-Time School Librarian Makes a Critical Difference in Boosting Student Achievement," *School Library Journal* 59, no. 3 (March 2013): 28.

5. Keith Curry Lance and Bill Schwartz, "How Pennsylvania School Libraries Pay Off: Investments in Student Achievement and Academic Standards" (PA School Library Project, 2012), cited by Mary K. Biagini, "How Do School Libraries Help Pennsylvania Students Achieve Academic Success? What School Library Advocates Need to Know" (PA School Library Project, October 2012): 6.

6. David V. Loertscher and Kathryn Roots Lewis, "Implementing the Common Core State Standards: The Role of the School Librarian" (Chicago: Achieve and American Association of School Librarians, November 2013): 8.

7. Judi Moreillon, *Coteaching Reading Comprehension Strategies in Elementary School Libraries: Maximizing Your Impact* (Chicago: ALA, 2013); Judi Moreillon, *Coteaching Reading Comprehension Strategies in Secondary School Libraries: Maximizing Your Impact* (Chicago: ALA, 2012); AASL, "The School Librarian's Role in Reading Toolkit," http://www.ala.org/aasl/advocacy/tools/toolkits/role-reading.

8. Karen Wixson, "Assessment and Instruction in the Era of the CCSS in English Language Arts," April 24, 2013, Common Core State Standards Webinar Series, Text Project, http://textproject.org/archive/webinars/common-core-state-standards-webinar-series-2/key-shifts-in-assessment-and-instruction-related-to-ccss-ela.

9. Loertscher and Lewis, "Implementing the Common Core State Standards"; Ruth Uecker, Shelly Kelly, and Marni Napierela, "Implementing the Common Core State Standards: What Is the School Librarian's Role?," *Knowledge Quest* 42, no. 3 (February 2014): 48–51.

10. Michelle Kelley and Nicki Clausen-Grace, "R5: The Sustained Silent Reading Makeover That Transformed Readers," *The Reading Teacher* 60, no. 2 (2006): 148. doi:10.1598/RT.60.2.5.

11. Rachael E. Allington and Richard L. Gabriel, "Every Child, Every Day," *Educational Leadership* 69, no. 6 (March 2012): 10.

12. Loertscher and Lewis, "Implementing the Common Core State Standards: The Role of the School Librarian," 9.

13. Kelley and Clausen-Grace, "R5."

14. Pam Allyn, "Taming the Wild Text," *Educational Leadership* 69, no. 6 (March 2012): 16–21.

15. Douglas Fisher and Nancy Frey, "Close Reading in Elementary Schools," *The Reading Teacher* 66, no. 3 (2012): 179–88, doi:10.1002/TRTR.01117.

16. Julie Harris, "Expanding the School Library Media Specialist's Role: Integrating Close Reading Activities into the Library Curriculum," *Library Media Connection* 32, no. 4 (February 2014): 14–16.

17. Fisher and Frey, "Close Reading in Elementary Schools."

18. "Special Issue: CCSS and Inquiry," *School Library Monthly* 29, no. 4 (January 2013); Uecker, Kelly, and Napierela, "Implementing the Common Core State Standards: What Is the School Librarian's Role?"; Loertscher and Lewis, "Implementing the Common Core State Standards: The Role of the School Librarian"; Mary Ann Wolf, Rachel Jones, and Daniel Gilbert, "Leading in and Beyond the Library" (Washington, DC: Alliance for Excellent Education, January 2014).

19. Taffy E. Raphael, "Teaching Question-Answer Relationships, Revisited," *The Reading Teacher* 39, no. 6 (February 1986): 516–522, cited by Fisher and Frey, "Close Reading in Elementary Schools"; Christine Walker and Sarah Shaw, *Teaching Reading Strategies in the School Library* (Westport, CT: Libraries Unlimited, 2004).

20. Walker and Shaw, *Teaching Reading Strategies in the School Library.*

21. Wixson, "Assessment and Instruction in the Era of the CCSS in English Language Arts."

22. Ibid.

23. Doug Johnson, "Common Sense Economy," Doug-Johnson.com, January 2005; Buffy Hamilton, "The Ultimate Classroom Library: Your School Media Center," *AASL Blog*, April 26, 2009.

24. National Governors Association Center for Best Practices, Council of Chief State School Officers, "Common Core State Standards, English Language Arts Standards."

25. Moreillon, *Coteaching Reading Comprehension Strategies in Secondary School Libraries.*

26. Sue Thomas et al., "Transliteracy: Crossing Divides," *First Monday* 12, no. 12 (December 12, 2007), http://firstmonday.org/ojs/index.php/fm/article/view/2060.

27. Gail Bush, "The Transliterate Learner," *School Library Monthly* 29, no. 1 (2012): 5–7.

Chapter 4

1. Adele Flynn (first-grade teacher, Newton, MA), interview with author, September 10, 2014.

2. Carol Kuhlthau, Leslie Maniotes, and Ann Caspari, *Guided Inquiry: Learning in the 21st Century* (Westport, CT: Libraries Unlimited, 2007), 133, cited by Annette Lamb and Daniel Callison, *Graphic Inquiry* (Denver: Libraries Unlimited, 2012).

3. Barbara K. Stripling, "Inquiry-Based Learning," in *Curriculum Connections Through the Library*, eds. Barbara K. Stripling and Sandra Hughes-Hassell (Westport, CT: Libraries Unlimited, 2003), 5.

4. Kuhlthau, Maniotes, and Caspari, *Guided Inquiry*, cited by Lamb and Callison, *Graphic Inquiry*, 11.

5. The following resources provide a deeper examination of inquiry: Jean Donham, "Inquiry," in *Inquiry and the Common Core*, eds. Violet H. Harada and Sharon

Coatney (Santa Barbara, CA: Libraries Unlimited, 2014), 3–15; Carol C. Kuhlthau, Leslie K. Maniotes, and Ann K. Caspari, *Guided Inquiry Design: A Framework for Inquiry in Your School* (Santa Barbara, CA: Libraries Unlimited, 2012); Lamb and Callison, *Graphic Inquiry*; Randell K. Schmidt, *A Guided Inquiry Approach to High School Research* (Santa Barbara, CA: Libraries Unlimited, 2013); Virginia L. Wallace and Whitney Norwood Husid, *Collaborating for Inquiry-Based Learning: School Librarians and Teachers Partner for Student Achievement* (Denver: Libraries Unlimited, 2011); Daniel Callison, "Information Literacy to Inquiry: A Timeline," *School Library Monthly* 31, no. 1 (October 2014): 15–25.

6. Stripling, "Inquiry-Based Learning"; Barbara Stripling, "Inquiry: Inquiring Minds Want to Know," *School Library Monthly* 35, no. 1 (September 2008): 50–52.

7. Barbara K. Stripling, "Inquiry-Based Learning," 7.

8. Kuhlthau, Maniotes, and Caspari, *Guided Inquiry Design*, xiii.

9. Ibid.

10. Carol C. Kuhlthau and Leslie K. Maniotes, "Building Guided Inquiry Teams for 21st-Century Learners," *School Library Monthly* 26, no. 5 (January 2010): 18–21.

11. Michael B. Eisenberg and Robert E. Berkowitz, "Big6 Skills Overview," 2013, http://big6.com/pages/about/big6-skills-overview.php.

12. Mike Eisenberg, Doug Johnson, and Bob Berkowitz, "Information, Communications, and Technology (ICT) Skills Curriculum Based on the Big6 Skills Approach to Information Problem-Solving," *Library Media Connection* 28, no. 6 (May/June 2010): 27.

13. Carol Doll, *Collaboration and the School Library Media Specialist* (Lanham, MD: Scarecrow Press, 2005), 31.

14. Patricia Montiel-Overall and Kim Grimes, "Teachers and Librarians Collaborating on Inquiry-Based Science Instruction: A Longitudinal Study," *Library & Information Science Research* 35, no. 1 (January 2013): 48.

15. Flynn, interview with author.

16. Stripling, "Inquiry-Based Learning," 6.

17. David V. Loertscher, Carol Koechlin, and Sandi Zwaan, *Ban Those Bird Units* (Salt Lake City: Hi Willow Research and Publishing, 2005).

18. Ibid.

19. Ibid., xxv.

20. Michael Scriven and Richard Paul, "Defining Critical Thinking," Foundation for Critical Thinking, 2008, http://www.criticalthinking.org/pages/defining-critical-thinking/410, cited by Jennifer Wilson Mulnix, "Thinking Critically About Critical Thinking," *Educational Philosophy and Theory* 44, no. 5 (2012): 465.

21. Mulnix, "Thinking Critically About Critical Thinking," 465.

22. AASL, *Standards for the 21st-Century Learner in Action* (Chicago: ALA, 2009), 61.

23. CIBER, "Information Behaviour of the Researcher of the Future," University College London, March 1, 2010, http://www.ucl.ac.uk/infostudies/research/ciber/.

24. AASL, *Standards for the 21st-Century Learner in Action.*

25. Debra S. Peterson and Barbara M. Taylor, "Using Higher Order Questioning to Accelerate Students' Growth in Reading," *The Reading Teacher* 65, no. 5 (2012): 295–304, doi:10.1002/TRTR.01045.

26. Lois Lowry, *Number the Stars* (Boston: Houghton Mifflin Co., 1989).

27. AASL, *Standards for the 21st-Century Learner in Action*, 17.

28. Pam Berger, "Student Inquiry and Web 2.0," *School Library Monthly* 26, no. 5 (January 2010): 14–17.

Chapter 5

1. Violet H. Harada and Joan M. Yoshina, *Assessing for Learning: Librarians and Teachers as Partners*, 2nd ed. (Westport, CT: Libraries Unlimited, 2010), 9.

2. Ibid., 10–12.

3. Rick Stiggins and Jan Chappuis, "What a Difference a Word Makes," *Journal of Staff Development* 27, no. 1 (Winter 2006): 11.

4. AASL, *Standards for the 21st-Century Learner* (Chicago: ALA, 2007).

5. AASL, *Standards for the 21st-Century Learner in Action* (Chicago: ALA, 2009), 9.

6. Harada and Yoshina, *Assessing for Learning*.

7. Geography Education National Implementation Project, "National Geography Standard: Geography Standard 4: The Physical and Human Characteristics of Places," NationalGeographic.com, Education, 2014, http://education.nationalgeographic.com/education/standards/national-geography-standards/4/?ar_a=1.

8. AASL, *Standards for the 21st-Century Learner*.

9. Janice Gilmore-See, *Simply Indispensable: An Action Guide for School Librarians* (Santa Barbara, CA: Libraries Unlimited, 2010), 60–61.

10. Ibid., 61–62.

11. Jan Chappuis, "How Am I Doing?," *Educational Leadership* 70, no. 1 (September 1, 2012): 37.

12. Ibid.

13. Interview with author: Thomas Lesniewski (assistant superintendent of 6–12 curriculum and instruction, East Stroudsberg Area School District, PA). February 13, 2014.

14. Kent State University Libraries, "TRAILS: Tool for Real-Time Assessment of Information Literacy Skills," 2014, http://www.trails-9.org/about2.php?page=about.

15. Marla McGhee and Barbara A. Jansen, *The Principal's Guide to a Powerful Library Media Program: A School Library for the 21st Century*, 2nd ed. (Denver: Linworth, 2010), 98.

16. Lesley Farmer, "Principals: Catalysts for Collaboration," *School Libraries Worldwide* 13, no. 1 (January 2007): 64.

17. Keith Curry Lance and Debra E. Kachel, "Achieving Academic Standards Through the School Library Program: Administrator Perceptions and Student Test Scores," *Teacher Librarian* 40, no. 5 (June 2013): 10.

18. Keith Curry Lance and Bill Schwartz, "How Pennsylvania School Libraries Pay Off: Investments in Student Achievement and Academic Standards," 2012.

19. Lance and Kachel, "Achieving Academic Standards Through the School Library Program"

20. Jesse Turner (principal, Monticello High School, Albemarle County Public Schools, VA), interview with author, February 21, 2014.

21. Erik Burmeister, "Why Not Say Yes?" *Principal Leadership* 14, no. 6 (February 2014): 60.

22. Jean Donham, "Assignments Worth Doing," *School Library Monthly* 28, no. 2 (November 2011): 7.

Chapter 6

1. Kafi Kumasi-Johnson, "Critical Inquiry: Library Media Specialists as Change Agents," in *21st-Century Learning in School Libraries*, ed. Kristin Fontichiaro (Denver: Libraries Unlimited, 2009), 151.

2. Kumasi-Johnson, "Critical Inquiry," 151, citing Judith J. Slater, Stephen M. Fain, and Caesar A. Rossatto, *The Freirean Legacy: Educating for Social Justice* (New York: Peter Lang Publishing, 2002).

3. Ibid., 152.

4. Cynthia Kanaroi (principal, Marshall Middle School, North Allegheny School District, Wexford, PA), interview with author, May 28, 2014.

5. Pura Belpré's story is told in the Spanish and English picture book *The Storyteller's Candle/La Velita de los Cuentos*, written by Lucia González and illustrated by Lulu Delacre. This book was chosen as an Honor Book for the literature award named for Pura Belpré. Given by the Association for Library Service to Children (ALSC), a division of ALA and REFORMA, an ALA affiliate, the Pura Belpré Award, "established in 1996, is presented annually to a Latino/Latina writer and illustrator whose work best portrays, affirms, and celebrates the Latino cultural experience in an outstanding work of literature for children and youth." ALSC, "Welcome to the Pura Belpré Award Home Page!," ALA.org, 2014, http://www.ala.org/alsc/awardsgrants/bookmedia/belpremedal.

6. Bonnie Mackey and Sharon Pitcher, "Family Literacy: The Dynamic Roles School Librarians Can Play," in *School Reform and the School Library Media Specialist*, eds. Sandra Hughes-Hassell and Violet H. Harada, Principles and Practice Series (Westport, CT: Libraries Unlimited, 2007), 82.

7. Carrie Scott Banks et al., *Including Families of Children with Special Needs*, rev. ed. (Chicago: Neal-Schuman Publishers, 2014).

8. Denise E. Agosto and Sandra Hughes-Hassell, "Language, Culture, and the School Library," in *School Reform and the School Library Media Specialist*, eds. Sandra Hughes-Hassell and Violet H. Harada, Principles and Practice Series (Westport, CT: Libraries Unlimited, 2007), 147–148, citing Denise E. Agosto, "The Cultured Word: Cultural Background, Bilingualism, and the School Library," *School Libraries Worldwide* 7, no. 1 (2001): 46–57.

9. Andrew J. M. Smith and Nancy J. Brown, "Crossing the Language Barrier: The Potential for School Librarians in Facilitating Cross-Cultural Teaching and Learning

in the School Library," in *School Libraries Matter: Views from the Research*, ed. Mirah J. Dow (Denver: Libraries Unlimited, 2013), 137–49.

10. Nancy Everhart and Marcia Mardis, "What Do Stakeholders Know About School Library Programs? Results of a Focus Group Evaluation," *School Library Research* 17 (February 2014): 10.

11. Laura L. Summers, "Culturally Responsive Leadership in School Libraries," *Library Media Connection* 28, no. 5 (March 1, 2010): 12.

12. Ibid.

13. Banks et al., *Including Families of Children with Special Needs.*

14. Public Relations Society of America, "What Is Public Relations? PR Definition: PRSA Official Statement," PRSA.org, 2014.

15. Stephanie Harvey and Anne Goudvis, *Strategies That Work: Teaching Comprehension for Understanding and Engagement* (Portland, ME: Stenhouse Publishers, 2007), 17.

16. Cathy Allen Simon, "Strategy Guide: Making Connections," ReadWriteThink, 2014, http://www.readwritethink.org/professional-development/strategy-guides/making-connections-30659.html.

17. National Governors Association Center for Best Practices and Council of Chief State School Officers, "Common Core State Standards, English Language Arts Standards" (Washington, DC: National Governors Association Center for Best Practices, Council of Chief State School Officers, 2010), 7.

18. Ibid., 22.

19. Search Institute, "Developmental Assets: Preparing Young People for Success," Search Institute, 2014, http://www.search-institute.org/what-we-study/developmental-assets.

20. Ibid.

21. Rebecca Morris and Katelyn Nelson, "New Collaborations Though Effective Communication," *School Library Monthly* 30, no. 6 (March 2014): 11–12.

22. Cherie P. Pandora and Stacey Hayman, *Better Serving Teens Through School Library–Public Library Collaborations*, Libraries Unlimited Professional Guides for Young Adult Librarians Series (Denver: Libraries Unlimited, 2013).

Chapter 7

1. AASL, *Standards for the 21st-Century Learner in Action* (Chicago: ALA, 2009), 61.

2. David V. Loertscher et al., *The New Learning Commons: Where Learners Win!*, 2nd ed. (Salt Lake City: Learning Commons Press, 2011), 11.

3. Karen Gavigan, Shana Pribesh, and Gail Dickinson, "Fixed or Flexible Schedule? Schedule Impacts and School Library Circulation," *Library & Information Science Research* 32, no. 2 (April 2010): 131–137, doi:10.1016/j.lisr.2009.10.005.

4. Carolyn M. Jackson, "The High School Library Web Site: Scaffolding Information Literacy Skills" (EdD diss., Illinois State University, 2006).

5. Joyce Kasman Valenza, "Discovering a Descriptive Taxonomy of Attributes of Exemplary School Library Websites" (PhD diss., University of North Texas, 2007), 127.

6. American Library Association, "Access to Resources and Services in the School Library Media Program," accessed November 20, 2014, http://www.ala.org/advocacy/intfreedom/librarybill/interpretations/accessresources.

7. Mark Edwards, *Every Child, Every Day* (New York: Pearson, 2014).

8. Pam Berger, "Student Inquiry and Web 2.0," *School Library Monthly* 26, no. 5 (January 2010): 14.

9. Carol Doll, *Collaboration and the School Library Media Specialist* (Lanham, MD: Scarecrow Press, 2005).

10. Ibid., 59.

11. AASL, *School Libraries Count! National Longitudinal Survey of School Library Programs* (Chicago: ALA, 2012).

12. Donna M. Shannon, "Perceptions of School Library Programs and School Librarians: Perspectives of Supportive School Administrators," *Teacher Librarian* 39, no. 3 (2012): 18.

13. Charlotte Danielson, "Evaluations That Help Teachers Learn," *The Effective Educator* 68, no. 4 (January 12, 2010): 39.

14. Deborah Levitov, "Perspectives of School Administrators Related to School Libraries," in *School Libraries Matter: Views from the Research*, ed. Mirah J. Dow (Denver: Libraries Unlimited, 2013), 98.

15. The Danielson Group, "The Framework," 2013, http://danielsongroup.org/framework/.

16. Danielson, "Evaluations That Help Teachers Learn"; The Danielson Group, "The Framework."

17. Patricia Owen, *A 21st-Century Approach to School Librarian Evaluation* (Chicago: AASL, 2012); American Association for School Librarians and Brittanica Digital Learning, *A Planning Guide for Empowering Learners*, http://www.ala.org/aasl/standards-guidelines/planning-guide.

18. American Association of School Librarians and Association for Educational Communications and Technology, *Information Power: Building Partnerships for Learning* (Chicago: ALA, 1998).

Chapter 8

1. Interviews with author: Scott Bacon (principal, Blue Valley High School, Johnson County, KS), February 20, 2014; Justin Zona (director of curriculum, Fairview School District, Erie County, PA), February 10, 2014; Jesse Turner (principal, Monticello High School, Albemarle County Public Schools, VA), February 21, 2014; Thomas Lesniewski (assistant superintendent of 6–12 curriculum and instruction, East Stroudsberg Area School District, PA), February 13, 2014.

2. Turner, interview.

3. Massachusetts Department of Elementary and Secondary Education, "Regulations for Educator Licensure and Preparation Program Approval," December 26, 2012, 14, http://www.doe.mass.edu/lawsregs/603cmr7.html?section=10.

4. Gail Bush and Jami L. Jones, "Exploration to Identify Professional Dispositions of School Librarians: A Delphi Study," *School Library Media Research* 13 (January 2010).

5. Jami L. Jones, "Promoting Resilience: Ways Library Media Specialists Strengthen Children," *School Library Media Activities Monthly* 32, no. 3 (November 2005): 25–27.

6. Gail Munde, "Caring for Your Tribe," *Knowledge Quest* 40, no. 5 (June 5, 2012): 26.

7. John D. Crowley, *Developing a Vision: Strategic Planning for the School Librarian in the 21st Century*, 2nd ed. (Denver: Libraries Unlimited, 2011).

8. Mary K. Biagini, "The Pennsylvania Story: Lessons Learned," *School Library Monthly* 30, no. 5 (February 2014): 6.

9. Deborah Detenbeck Levitov, "Perspectives of School Administrators Related to School Library Media Programs After Participating in an Online Course, 'School Library Advocacy for Administrators'" (PhD diss., University of Missouri–Columbia, 2009), 136.

10. Debra E. Kachel and Keith Curry Lance, "Librarian Required: A New Study Shows That a Full-Time School Librarian Makes a Critical Difference in Boosting Student Achievement," *School Library Journal* 59, no. 3 (March 2013): 28.

11. American Association for School Librarians Advocacy Committee, "What Is Advocacy?" n.d., http://www.ala.org/aasl/advocacy/definitions.

12. Bradley Portin, "School-Based Leadership in the U.S. in an Age of Reform: What Does It Take?," *Education Research and Perspectives* 32, no. 2 (2005): 1–23.

ACKNOWLEDGMENTS

I owe great thanks to the school principals, teachers, librarians, and administrators who shared conversations with me during their busy school days. Their stories and enthusiasm for school libraries were informative and inspiring!

Thank you to Brita Zitin and Matt Weber for thinking of me when you wanted to make an HGSE *EdCast* about school libraries. Your idea set this project into motion. Thank you to my editor, Caroline Chauncey, for your warm energy, careful insights, and trust.

I am grateful to have outstanding mentors and colleagues in school libraries, education, and library science whom I admire as leaders and learners. Thank you for the example you put forth and the work that you have done for students, school communities, and, of course, school librarians.

Thank you, school librarians, for being the heart of your schools.

ABOUT THE AUTHOR

REBECCA J. MORRIS, PHD, is an assistant professor in the Department of Library and Information Studies of the School of Education, University of North Carolina at Greensboro. She earned her doctoral and master's degrees at the University of Pittsburgh. Rebecca holds a Bachelor of Science degree from The Pennsylvania State University.

Rebecca has a professional background as an elementary classroom teacher and school librarian. She currently teaches graduate courses in school library curriculum, children's materials and services, and digital media production. Her research interests include educational preparation of school librarians and digital storytelling.

She is an active member and committee leader within the American Association of School Librarians, a division of the American Library Association. Rebecca and her husband, Brian, live in Charlotte, North Carolina.

INDEX

AASL. *See* American Association of School Librarians (AASL)
academic outcomes, 139–141
  school library positive impact on, 178
academic standards, 1
achievement gap, 23–24
active listening, 96–97
Activism and the School Librarian: Tools for Advocacy and Survival, 179
administrators
  academic standards, 120
  aligning school and state curricula, 173
  communicating with librarians, 119–121
  engaging all students, 173
  evaluating school librarians, 120, 164
  key library practices value, 120
  library as focal point of schools, 171–172
  promoting meaningful assessments, 119–123
  responsibilities and mission of school libraries, 179–184
  saying yes to librarian-teacher collaboration, 121
  school library advocacy, 177
Agosto, Denise, 133
aides in school libraries, 9
Alliance for Excellent Education, 50, 51
American Association of School Librarians (AASL), 8, 69
  Best Apps for Teaching and Learning, 160
  Common Beliefs, 11–20
  A Planning Guide for Empowering Learners: With School Library Program Assessment Rubric, 166
  policies and practices, 11–12
  school librarians, 29
  School Libraries Count! Survey, 163
  Standards for the 21st-Century Learner, 11–12, 81, 94, 110, 118, 141–142
  A 21st-Century Approach to School Librarian Evaluation, 166
  Top Websites for Teaching and Learning, 160
American Library Association, 4
  American Association of School Librarians (AASL), 11
arguments and text-based evidence, 74–75
Assessing for Learning: Librarians and Teachers as Partners (Harada and Yoshina), 106
assessment for learning, 26
  collaboration arc, 108–115
  collaborative assessment planning, 108–111
  collaborative instruction and assessment, 111–113
  concluding projects, 113–115

assessment for learning (*continued*)
fourth-grade social studies inquiry, 103–105
overview, 105–106
school libraries, 107
student assessment, 106, 113–115
teachers' assessment, 106
Assessment Planner workshop, 114
Assessment Product workshop, 114
assessments
administrators promoting meaningful, 119–123
collaborative instruction and, 111–114
collecting library data, 117–118
designing and implementing, 115–119
educators and, 105
inquiries, 119
librarian and teacher evaluation, 115, 118–119
library class check-ins, 116–117
longitudinal assessment, 118
peer sharing, 110
reflecting on, 113–115
stars and stairs feedback, 116
that's good, now this framework, 116
assignments
design, 91–94
inquiry-based characteristics, 85
"Assignments Worth Doing," 122
authentic audiences, 129–130
Authentic Intellectual Work framework, 122
authors, truth in representing ideas of, 19

Bacon, Scott, 171
Banks, James, 134
Ban Those Bird Units (Loertscher et al.), 92
Belpré, Pura, 132
Berger, Pam, 100–101, 160
Bergmann, Jonathan, 49
Berkowitz, Robert, 89
Best Apps for Teaching and Learning, 160
Better Serving Teens Through School Library-Public Library Collaborations (Pandora and Hayman), 144
Big6 model, 89
bird units, 92
bit.ly, 47
blended learning, 8, 15
Blendspace, 47
Blue Valley High School, 48
books, 9, 13
bridges to school priorities, 11–12
collaborative, accountable communities of learners, 18–20, 36, 174–176
interdisciplinary learning, 37
links across content areas, 15–16, 173–174
reading gateway to the world, 12–14
social context of learning, 14
transliteracy skills, 16–18, 174
Burmeister, Erik, 122
Bush, Gail, 42, 80

career learning, 35
Caspari, Ann, 89
CCSS. *See* Common Core State Standards (CCSS)
Church, Audrey, 23
citizenship, 1
classroom libraries, 77
classrooms
applying literacies to, 17–18
school library website as home page, 129
close reading, 73–76
collaboration, 11
different forms and depths, 162

learning commons, 42
library programs, 177
literacy instruction, 67
maximizing opportunities for, 162
maximum student learning, 116
planning and reflection, 163
rating effectiveness of, 114
school librarians, 6
schoolwide strategies, 161–162
students, 42
trust and legwork, 122
Collaboration and the School Library Media Specialist (Doll), 161
collaboration arc, 85
assessment for learning, 108–115
collaborative assessment planning, 108–111
collaborative culture in school, 90
content, 90
information literacy instruction, 91
inquiry-based science, 91
collaborative assessment planning, 108–111
collaborative culture in school, 90
collaborative instruction and assessment, 111–113
collection development, 13
collection management, 44–46
Common Beliefs
equitable access to education, 18–20
ethical behavior in use of information, 18–20
information demands and thinking skills, 16–18
information literacy, 14–18
inquiry framework for learning, 15–16
reading as foundational skill, 62
reading gateway to the world, 12–14, 15–16
school libraries and developing learning skills, 15–16
social context of learning, 14, 18–20
technology skills and future employment, 16–18
Common Core State Standards (CCSS), 25
dialogue-style discussions, 140–141
evidence demonstrating learning, 66
grades 6–12 standards, 77–78
informational text, 81
instructional and assessment shifts, 69–70
K–5 ELA standards, 76–77
library programs, 39
literacy instruction responsibilities, 59–60
literacy learning, 77
literary texts, 66
other perspectives and cultures, 39
preparing students for, 107
reading complex texts, 65–66
text-based evidence, 74–75
valuing evidence, 39
communities
authentic engagement with, 125–145
business financial support for technology, 159
citizenship and social justice, 1
civic pride and unity from schools, 138
community reading programs, 141–143
diversity, 83–86
learning commons, 42
reading and reaching out to groups, 139
school libraries and, 136, 138–143
schools creating dividing lines in, 138
communities of learners, collaborative and accountable, 18–20, 174–176
community learning grants, 125–127
community reading programs, 136
academic outcomes, 139–141

community reading programs (*continued*)
  community outcomes, 141–143
  Developmental Assets framework, 141–143
  intergenerational and cross-cultural conversations, 139–140
  relationships with adults other than parents, 142
  respect for others' interpretations and questions, 141
competency-based projects, 11
concluding projects, 113–115
constructivism, 87
constructivist-based process of learning, 86–87
content
  background knowledge, 78–79
  curation, 44
  richness across resources, 7–8
content-based informational texts, 76–79
content-based instructional texts, 59
content-specific instructional guides, 45
contexts, applying literacies to, 17–18
co-teaching
  reading, 58–59
  school librarians, 5
Creating Innovators: The Making of Young People Who Will Change the World (Wagner), 34
critical inquiry, 129–130
critical thinking, 26, 94–95
  developing, 119
  inquiries, 84
cross-disciplinary connections, 1
cultural responsiveness, 134–136
curated digital collection, 45–46
curation
  collections, 47
  content, 44
  digital tools, 45–46
  multimedia content, 45
  resources, 44–46
  social, 46
  technology, 44–46
  vertical files, 44–45
curation tools, 47
curriculum
  focused on literacy learning, 65
  reading across, 57–82

Delicious, 47
Developmental Assets framework, 141–143
Dewey, John, 87
diagnostic assessment, 109
digital badging, 48
  individual learning experiences, 50–53
  Mozilla, 50–51
  self-assessment, 51
  teachers, 52
digital curation, 45–46
digital learning, 1, 160
digital media, 39
digital storytelling, 32
digital tools, 45–46
diverse-background families, 131–136
diverse needs
  community learning grants, 125–127
  cultural responsiveness, 134–136
  English language learners, 133–134
  families from diverse backgrounds, 131–136
  families serving as authentic audiences, 129–130
  family connections with school library, 127–130
  independent reading and information use, 130
  responding to, 26–27, 125–145, 132–133
diversity, 83–86
Doll, Carol, 161
Donham, Jean, 38, 122

"Drop Everything and Read" (DEAR) sessions, 63
dynamic school libraries, 27

education
 equitable access, 18–20
 school librarians, 2
 school libraries contributions, 1
 technology, 19
educators
 assessment, 105
 collaboration arc, 90–91
 inquiry, 90–94
Edwards, Mark, 42, 48, 159
Eisenberg, Michael, 89
elementary school libraries, 156
 fixed-flex schedule, 153–154
 fixed schedule, 152
 flexible schedule, 152–153
 setup, 151–152
English language arts (ELA)
 grades 6–12 standards and literacy instruction, 59
 service learning in makerspaces, 31–33
English language arts (ELA) teachers, 65
English language arts (ELA) teams, 64
English language learners, 133–134
equitable access to education, 18–20
ethical behavior in use of information, 18–20
Every Child, Every Day (Edwards), 42

fab labs, 33
Fadel, Charles, 28
fake readers, 71
families
 authentic audiences, 129–130
 authentic engagement with, 125–145
 children's reading needs, 131–132
 cultural background, 131–132
 diverse backgrounds, 131–136
 independent reading and information use, 130
 information about childrens' needs, 127
 literacy, 132
 school and school library involvement, 131–132
 school libraries connections, 127–130
 volunteering, 131
Farmer, Leslie, 119–120
feedback, 116
First Monday (Thomas et al.), 79–80
flexible access to learning commons, 43–44
flipped classrooms, 8
flipped instruction
 content normally taught in classroom, 49–50
 homework learning activities, 49
 library lessons, 50
 school library resources, 49–50
 teacher-developed instructional segment, 48–49
 teachers, 52
Flynn, Adele, 86, 91
formative assessment, 109–110, 114, 117
 learning appropriate for, 123
 receptiveness to constructive feedback, 113
fourth-grade social studies inquiry process assessment, 103–105
Framework for Teaching, 165
free web, 7

Gilmore-See, Janice, 114
Gordon, Carol, 24
"Graduating Students Who Are Not Only Learned But Also Learners," 38
Guided Inquiry, 89

hackerspaces, 33
health and physical education teachers, 66

higher-order questions, 74
high school health example, 100
high school library flexible schedules, 154–155
homework focused through recommended resources, 128–129
Hughes-Hassell, Sandra, 133
hybrid learning, 8
Hyman, Shannon, 53

Implementing the Common Core State Standards: The Role of the School Librarian (Loertscher and Roots), 68
independent learning in satellite study hall, 48
independent reading, 130
information
  access to, 157–159
  demands and thinking skills, 16–18
  digital tools for sharing, 46
  ethical behavior in use of, 18–20
  families supporting use, 130
  honoring privacy, 19
  intended audience, 19
  interacting with, 108
informational texts
  Common Core State Standards (CCSS), 81
  content background knowledge, 78–79
  information-seeking skills, 78–79
  note taking, 79
  reading strategies, 78–79
information literacy, 14–17
  complex definition of, 16–18
  instruction, 91
  progress on longitudinal basis, 118
  school librarians as teacher of, 23
Information Power school library standards (1998), 168
information search process (ISP), 89
information-seeking skills, 78–79
information skills, 7
  carrying through later grades, 108
  practicing in context, 16
  subject-area content connections with, 15–16
information sources
  attributing appropriately and accurately, 19
  transliteracy skills, 16–18
information specialists, 6–8
inquiry, 26, 119
  assessments, 119
  assignment design, 91–94
  authentic audiences, 129–130
  background knowledge and course of action, 88
  Big6 model, 89
  versus bird units, 92
  building skills, 96–97
  classroom dialogue, 96–97
  collaboration arc, 85, 90–91
  connecting students in shared but individual processes, 93
  constructing questions, 84, 86, 92–93, 96–97
  constructivist-based process of learning, 86–87
  critical, 129–130
  critical thinking skills, 84, 94–95
  defining problem or question, 88
  educators, 90–94
  engaging students, 84
  finding bad article, 95
  fourth-grade social studies inquiry, 103–105
  framework for learning, 15–16
  Guided Inquiry, 89
  high school health example, 100
  identifying and evaluating sources, 88
  intention, 86
  interacting and using information, 88

interacting with texts and showing learning, 94
interdisciplinary learning and, 16
learning experiences and assignment characteristics, 85
lifelong learning, 87
local and global contexts, 1
motivating thread of content, 94
1:1 learning settings, 92
overview, 86–87, 90
project differences, 93
questioning, 94–97
recursive navigation, 88
reflection, 86
research models, 88–89
resources and technologies curation, 44–46
school libraries, 86
schoolwide culture of, 86
second-grade cultural fair example, 97–98
self-assessing, 86
sixth-grade novel example, *Number the Stars*, 98–99
slowing down and being intentional, 92–93
steps toward, 100–101
Stripling model of inquiry, 88–89
students, 94–97
Super3 model, 89
technology-focused instruction, 93
thinking, 94–95

inquiry-based learning, 7, 26, 100–101, 119
inquiry-based science, 91
instruction
interdisciplinary, 35
school librarians, 5
instructional and organizational goals, 27
intellectual property, 19
interdisciplinary instruction, 35
interdisciplinary learning, 15–16, 37
Internet, 7
acceptable use policy, 159
school library website as home page, 128–129
invisible web, 7–8
ISP. *See* information search process (ISP)

Jones, Jami Biles, 55, 175

Kent State University Libraries, 118
King, Kendra, 122
Kuhlthau, Carol, 89
Kumasi-Johnson, Kafi, 129–130

learning
activities engaging students, 38
assessment for, 26
blended, 8, 15
constructivist-based process, 86–87
different opportunities for, 35
hybrid, 8
inquiry-based, 7, 15–16, 26, 85, 100–101
interdisciplinary, 15–16, 37
library-integrated, 15–16, 19
making visible, 43
opportunities for, 32
personalized, 15
problem-based, 7
problem-solving, 34
project-based, 7
school libraries, 15–16
social context, 14, 18–20
student-centered, 25, 31–55
technology-integrated, 22
vocational and career, 35
learning commons, 25
access to materials, 41, 44
attitude, 41
collaboration, 42
community, 42
configuration, 43

learning commons (*continued*)
flexible access, 43–44
honoring students' ideas, 54
implementation levels, 53–55
introducing approach to school, 53–54
layout, 40–41
making learning visible, 43
people involved in, 43
personalized learning, 46, 48–52, 54
resources, 43
schedules, 43–44
spaces for, 43
student-centered learning, 38–43
student equity and access, 42
student participation and accountability, 48
teacher buy-in, 41
technology equipment and networks, 40
tools for content curation, 44
transliteracy skills, 42
learning community, 19
learning spaces, 1
Learnist, 47
Lesniewski, Thomas, 117, 172
Leverage Your Library Program to Raise Test Scores, 23
Levitov, Deborah, 177
librarian-curated collections, 47
library blog, 4
library class check-ins, 116–117
library conferences, 150
library data and collecting assessments, 117–118
library databases, 75
library-embedded lessons, 6
library-integrated learning, 15–16, 19
Library Ladder of Resiliency, 175
library portal, 3
library programs, 10
aligning strategies with literacy instruction, 68–79
collaboration, 177
collection development, 167
Common Core State Standards (CCSS), 39
components, 22–23
contributions by others to, 177
evaluating, 163–167
feedback, 166–167
fitting into students and teachers needs, 11
fixed schedules, 155–156
flexible schedules, 155–156
fostering continuity, 87
innovation, 177
leadership sources, 28
literacy instruction, 65
narrowing achievement gap, 23–24
potential for learning, 28
practices expanding basic elements, 64
practicing competencies for college, 39
principal support, 24
reading, 25, 62
reading incentive programs, 23
rotational schedule, 155
schoolwide initiatives, 118
student learning, 22–23, 61
summer reading programs, 23
teaching and ongoing professional growth culture, 22
transliteracy, 174
tying together school needs and community, 126–127
library science, 2
library science teachers, 29
library websites, 3
accommodating many uses and users, 4
measuring traffic and analytics, 167
pathways for library resources and online tools, 158
lifelong learning, 87, 174

LIS (library and information science/ studies) university alumni groups, 137
List.ly, 47
literacy
  contexts, classes, or projects, 17–18
  curriculum focused on learning, 65
  developing in students, 60
  families, 132
  grades 6–12 English language arts (ELA) standards and, 59
  grant funding to support initiative, 125–127
  libraries strengthening, 59–61
  reading, language arts, and English class, 77
  teachers and librarians co-planning and co-teaching, 80–82
literacy coaches, 60, 65
literacy instruction
  aligning people for maximum, 65–68
  collaboration, 67
  Common Core State Standards (CCSS), 59–60
  content-based instructional texts, 59
  positioning library programs central to, 65
  purposeful, 67
  reading stamina, 59
  school libraries bridging, 78
  transliteracy in reading instruction, 59
literacy programs
  aligning library program strategies with, 68–79
  connections with school libraries, 61–65
  support, resource, and enrichment, 64
literacy teams, 64, 66–67
local professional networks, 137
Loertscher, David V., 41–42, 68
longitudinal assessment, 118
Lowry, Lois, 98

Makerspace.com website, 33
Makerspace Playbook: School Edition, 35
makerspaces, 25, 33–34
  across grade levels and subject areas, 40
  focused learning opportunity, 32
  interdisciplinary instruction, 35
  introducing approach to school, 53–54
  modeling possible uses of, 36
  motivating for students, 37–38
  novices and experts working together, 37
  physical spaces for, 34
  products for, 34
  service learning in, 31–33, 35–38
  starting with specific project, 37
  STEM (science, technology, engineering, and math) projects, 35
  student-centered learning, 33–38
  teachers roles in projects, 35
  testing ideas and materials, 36
  what students can do with what they know, 34
Manifesto of Creative Inquiry, 55
Maniotes, Leslie, 89
media centers, 62
media specialist, 29
metacognition skills, 72
middle school library flexible schedules, 154–155
mobile device labs, 48
MOOCs (massive open online courses), 8
Moreillon, Judi, 69, 79
Mozilla, 50–51
Mulnix, Jennifer, 94
"The Multiple Dimensions of Principal Involvement," 24
multiple literacies, 14, 16–18, 25

National Center for Family Literacy, 132
National Center for Literacy Education, 60

National Holocaust Memorial website, 99
networks, 40
note making, 79
note taking, 79
Number the Stars (Lowry), 98–99

1:1 initiatives, 48
online learning, 48
online tools
  best access and pathways for, 158
  guiding teachers and students on, 160
  Internet acceptable use policy, 159
  strategies for positive use, 128
  student privacy, 159

paper.li, 47
Partnership for Assessment of Readiness for College Careers (PARCC), 76, 107
pathfinders, 45
peer sharing, 110
Pennsylvania School Library Project, 61
people, aligning for maximum literacy instruction, 65–68
personalized learning, 15, 46, 48–52, 54
  digital badging, 48
  flipped instruction, 48–50
Pink, Daniel, 117
plagiarizing, 19
A Planning Guide for Empowering Learners: With School Library Program Assessment Rubric, 166
portals, 44
presentation, 113
Principal Leadership (Burmeister), 122
privacy, 19
problem-based learning, 7
problem-solving learning, 34
professional culture and school library advocacy, 177–179
professional development, 114
  LIS (library and information science/studies) university alumni groups, 137
  local professional networks, 137
  reading stamina, 57–59
  school librarians, 149–150
  teachers, 23
professional learning network (PLN), 166
professional webinar, 150
program administrator, 8–10, 18
project-based learning, 7
projects, applying literacies to, 17–18
public libraries and collaboration, 143–145
public relations, 138–139

questions
  developing, 96–97
  guiding students to construct good, 92–93
  higher-order, 97
  inquiry, 94–97
  text-based evidence to answer, 74–75

reading
  academic context and, 13
  academic outcomes, 139–141
  academic vocabulary, 69–70
  accuracy, 72
  across curriculum, 57–82
  close reading, 73–76
  complexity of texts, 69
  comprehension, 1
  co-teaching, 58–59
  dialogue-style discussions, 140–141
  "Drop Everything and Read" (DEAR) sessions, 63
  evidence from texts, 69
  fake readers, 71
  foundational skills, 59, 62
  high priority for, 59

informational texts, 78
libraries strengthening literacy efforts, 59–61
library programs, 25, 62
noting progress of, 73
personal information needs, 13
providing resources for, 58
reaching out to community groups, 139
recreational, 13
regurgitating what was read, 92
report style of, 92
students gaining value from experiences, 71–72
successful, 70–71
sustained silent reading (SSR), 71
talking with peers about, 72
teachers, 65–66
text-based evidence, 73–76
understanding, 72
window to the world, 12–14, 15–16
reading incentive programs, 23
reading instruction
daily elements, 72
transliteracy, 59, 79–82
reading programs training, 64
reading readiness barriers, 71
reading specialists, 65
reading stamina, 70–73
activities supporting, 57
awareness of what they are doing while reading, 72
content knowledge or story, 72
identity of students as readers, 72
literacy instruction, 59
metacognition skills, 72
modeling what good readers do, 73
multilevel goals, 72–73
noticing their thinking during reading, 72–73
positive reading experiences, 72
reading experiences value, 71–72
third-grade reading, 57–59
reading strategies, 78–80
reading teachers, 65, 68
ReadWriteThink strategy, 140
Reed, Jennifer, 43
reference databases, 7
Remodeling Literacy Learning report, 60
report/term paper, 92
rereading, 73, 74
research
finding bad article, 95
key words and concepts, 111
models and inquiry, 88–89
students choosing topic, 91–92
resources, 7–8
resources curation, 44–46
responsibility and students, 46, 48–52, 54
Roots, Kathryn, 68

Sams, Aaron, 49
satisficing, 95
school counselors, 66
school leaders
collection mapping, 173
connections with families, 126–130
coordination with school librarians, 64
facilitating access to libraries, 19
instructional and organizational goals, 27
librarians communicating with, 119–121
library assessment, 107
necessity for libraries, 2
positioning library program centrally to literacy instruction, 65
priority areas and school libraries, 1
role, 18–19
school librarians, 1, 10–11, 177
school librarians, 29, 66
academic vocabulary, 70

school librarians (*continued*)
American Association of School Librarians (AASL) policies and practices, 11–12
assessments, 115
balancing informational and literary texts, 70
book borrowing, 9
building trust, 135
carrying books at all times policy, 63
children's and young adult literature, 2
collaborative lessons, 15–16, 151
collection development, 13
collection mapping, 173
Common Core State Standards (CCSS), 70
communicating with administrators, 119–121
continuity of instruction, 173
continuous learning, 166
coordination with school leaders, 64
core competencies of, 4
co-teaching, 5
co-teaching reading, 58–59, 64
cross-grade-level expertise, 173
cultural awareness, 135
curriculum planning committees, 64
designing digital media and instructional materials, 2
disciplines knowledge, 70
disengagement in students, 71
district-adopted reading strategies for, 64
education, 2
evaluating, 118–119, 163–167
fostering motivation, 135
impact on student learning, 5
improving literacy learning, 60
information from variety of sources, 2
information specialists, 6–8, 133
instruction, 5
instructional partners, 6
interdisciplinary view of curriculum, 173
knowing and interacting with students, 175
leader role, 1, 18–19, 28
library science, 2
literacy initiatives, 60
local professional networks, 137
matching reading levels and interests, 58
materials for student learning, 12–14
multiple literacies, 2
planning and teaching literacy, 80–82
potential for learning, 28
professional development, 23, 149–150, 150
professional evaluation, 164–166
professional learning network (PLN), 166
program administrator, 8–10, 18
promoting reading, 12–14, 62–63
range of activities, 165
resources for reading, 58
roles, 4–11
schedules, 5, 155–157
school leaders, 10–11, 177
staircase of complexity, 70
standards-aligned curricula, 22
standards and, 64
Standards for the 21st-Century Learner, 11–12
stereotypes of, 2
student inclusion, 135
student learning, 165
talking to, 148
as teachers, 5–6, 23
teaching inquiry, 85
technology integration, 8, 22–23
text-based answers, 70
titles, 29
transliteracy, 17

working several buildings in district, 66–67
writing from sources, 70
"The School Librarian's Role in Reading Toolkit," 69
school libraries
academic success, 178
aides or volunteers, 9
assessment, 107
Authentic Intellectual Work framework, 122
best practices, 151
caring place, 174–176
versus classroom libraries, 77
collection, 23
commonalties, 3
communities and, 136, 138–143
communities of learners, 18–20
contributions to education, 1
diagnostic assessment, 109
diverse needs, 26–27, 132–133
diversity of content, 132
dynamic, 27
educational technology, 19
equity and access, 18–19
expectations for, 20–22
facilitating teacher collaboration, 161–163
family connections, 127–130
family resource center, 133
focal point of schools, 171–172
formative assessment, 109
homework focus, 128–129
impact of, 22–24
information and technology tools, 157–159
inquiry, 86
integration in schools, 27–28
interdisciplinary instruction, 35
interdisciplinary learning, 37
learning commons, 38
learning skills development, 15–16
library programs, 10
links across content areas, 15–16
literacy, 59–61
literacy instruction, 78
literacy programs, 61–65
management role, 8–10
materials for projects, 128
mission and threads, 179–184
necessity for, 1–2
online resources, 128
opportunities for learning, 35
personalized learning, 46, 48–52, 54
personal reading and information, 128
philosophies, 2
portals, 44
professional culture, 177–179
public library collaborations, 143–145
reading, 62–63
reading stamina, 70–73
recent standards, 17
relaxing rules, 149
resource center for materials, 62
resources and flipped instruction, 49–50
roles, 4–11
schedules, 43–44
school goals, 3, 42
school leaders, 28
school mission and culture, 24
school priorities, 28, 30
schoolwide reach, 61
self-assessment, 148–149
shared ownership, 175
social context of learning, 14
social learning community, 19
standards-aligned curricula, 22
strong, 171–172
student access to, 23
student learning, 28, 127–130, 151, 179–184
students in need, 176
summative assessment, 109

school libraries (*continued*)
talking to students and teachers about, 148
teaching and learning activities, 3
technology integration, 8
top ten steps to maximize, 147–151
transliteracy skills, 16–18
visiting other, 148
School Libraries Count! Survey, 163
"School Library Impact Studies: Research Summary," 22
School Library Research Summarized, 22, 23
school library schedules
elementary school fixed-flex schedule, 153–154
elementary school fixed schedule, 152
elementary school flexible schedule, 152–153
extending, 158–159
promoting librarian interaction, 155–157
promoting maximum student access, 155–157
secondary school mostly flexible schedule, 154–155
school library website as home page, 128–129
school principals, 20–21, 24
schools
bridges to priorities, 11–12, 14–20
citizenship and social justice, 1
civic pride and unity, 138
dividing lines in community, 138
library integration in, 27–28
programs relationship with, 15–20
public relations, 138–139
Scoop.lt, 47
Search Institute, 142
secondary school library, 156–157
flexible schedule, 154–155
mostly flexible schedule, 154–155
secondary students, 74–75
second-grade cultural fair example, 97–98
self-assessing, 86
benchmarks, 117
building skills, 96–97
digital badging, 51
schoolwide focus on, 148–149
self-questioning strategies, 130
schoolwide focus on, 148–149
service learning in makerspaces
bringing teachers into projects, 36
collaboration between librarian and teachers, 37
English language arts (ELA), 31–33
guiding students in information seeking and use, 36
teachers' roles in projects, 35
technology, 32
shared reflection, 114
sixth-grade novel example, *Number the Stars,* 98–99
Smarter Balanced Assessment Consortium, 76, 107
SMART (Specific, Measureable, Attainable, Realistic, and Timely) goals, 118–119, 164
social context of learning, 14, 18–20
social curation, 46
social justice, 1
social learning community, 19
social media, 32, 159
speaking
building skills, 96–97
grounded in evidence from texts, 69
special education teachers, 65, 66
specialist teachers, 66
Standards for the 21st-Century Learner, 11–12, 81, 142
Standards for the 21st-Century Learner (2007), 17, 110, 118

Standards for the 21st-Century Learner in Action, 96, 109
stars and stairs feedback, 116
A 21st-Century Approach to School Librarian Evaluation, 166
STEM (science, technology, engineering, and math) learning, 1
  makerspaces, 35
Stephenson, Chad, 43
Stripling, Barbara, 86–88, 91, 101
Stripling model of inquiry, 88–89, 101
student-centered learning, 25
  learning commons, 38–43
  makerspaces, 31–38
student-curated collections, 47
student learning
  amplifying school libraries for, 179–184
  central role of libraries in, 28
  equipping library with materials for, 12–14
  families viewing products of, 129–130
  flipped instruction, 48–50
  impact of school librarians on, 5
  library programs and, 23
  school libraries, 3, 127–130, 151
student policies for using their own devices, 48
students
  activities engaging minds, 38
  central partners in assessment, 106
  choosing topic for research, 91–92
  collaboration, 42
  comprehending as well as critiquing, 39
  connecting in shared but individual processes, 93
  constructing good questions, 92–93
  constructing questions to investigate, 84
  constructive feedback, 113
  digital learning, 1
  fear of bullying, 175–176
  independence and strong content knowledge, 39
  independently motivating thread of content, 94
  information search process (ISP), 89
  information seeking and use, 36
  information skills, 7
  inquiry, 94–97
  integrating library resources and strategies into search habits, 129
  interacting with texts and showing learning, 94
  library programs, 27
  materials reflecting diverse topics and formats, 41
  multiple literacies, 14
  online, 48
  peers and reading and writing, 72
  personalized learning, 46, 48–52, 54
  promoting learning, 1
  reading experiences value, 71–72
  reading foundational skill for achievement, 59
  responding to various demands, 39
  responsibility, 46, 48–52, 54
  safe places for, 1
  school libraries, 23, 155–157
  self-assessment, 110
  talking about school library with, 148
  technology and digital media, 39
  thinking and questioning, 94–97
  thinking during reading, 72–73
  topic building and extending classroom activities, 111
  transliteracy, 14, 36
  trust in co-teacher, 113
  what they can do with what they know, 34
subject-area content and information skills, 15–16

summative assessment, 109, 113–115, 123
summer reading programs, 23
  public library collaborations, 144
Super3 model, 89
sustained silent reading (SSR), 71

tasks fostering transliteracy skills, 16–18
teacher collaboration
  barriers, 161
  facilitating, 161–163
teachers
  assessment, 106
  bringing into projects, 36
  context-specific criteria for evaluations, 165
  co-teaching and co-planning reading, 64
  digital badging, 52
  digital learning, 1
  engaging all students, 173
  evaluation of, 118–119
  flipped instruction, 52
  information skills, 7
  learning commons buy-in, 41
  makerspace projects, 35
  multiple literacies, 14
  planning and teaching literacy with librarians, 80–82, 151
  professional development, 23
  reading, 65–66
  school librarians as, 5–6
  signing up for library visits, 4
  talking about school library with, 148
  transliteracy, 14
  working with students in unique settings and durations, 66
Teaching Reading Strategies in the School Library (Walker and Shaw), 74
technology
  complementing and contributing to integration of, 8
  curation, 44–46
  digital storytelling, 32
  education, 19
  equipment access, 40
  future employment skills, 16–18
  makerspaces, 32
  school librarians, 23
  social media, 32
  students using, 39
  tools access, 157–159
  transliteracy and, 80
technology-integrated learning, 22
technology specialists, 8
text
  content-based informational, 76–79
  interacting with, 73
  reading accurately, 72
text-based evidence, 73–76, 104
that's good, now this framework, 116
think-aloud strategies, 130, 149
thinking
  expansion of information demands, 16–18
  higher-order, 97
  innovative, entrepreneurial, 1
  inquiry, 94–95
third-grade reading, 57–59
top ten steps to maximize school libraries
  going into library and looking at it, 147–148
  talking to school librarian, 148
  talking to students about school library, 148
  visiting other libraries, 148
Top Websites for Teaching and Learning, 160
TRAILS (Tools for Real-Time Assessment of Information Literacy Skills) assessment tool, 118
transliteracy, 14, 16–18, 36, 42
  context-specific strategies, 80
  demonstrating literacies, 17
  library programs, 174

modes of engagement skills, 81
navigating information landscapes, 17
reading instruction, 59, 79–82
reading strategies, 80
school libraries fostering skills, 16–18
skills, 79–80
teaching, 17
technology and, 80
Trilling, Bernie, 28
trophy books, 71
Turner, Jesse, 37, 121, 171, 172

unified arts teachers, 66
University of Michigan School of Information's "Michigan Makers Team," 52

Valenza, Joyce, 45
vertical files, 44–45
The Virtual Learning Commons, 42
virtual library, 3
vocational learning, 35
VoiceThread, 52, 86
volunteers in school libraries, 9

Wagner, Tony, 34
writing
associated with close reading, 76
grounded in evidence from texts, 69
talking with peers about, 72

Zona, Justin, 171